An important note to readers

Although every effort has been made to ensure the accuracy and correctness of the information contained in this book, it may change at any time for many reasons, including market forces, political, legal and economic conditions. The author shall not be responsible for any loss or damage experienced by readers resulting in errors in information or omissions from this book.

Amazon Publishing

© 2016 by Trevor J. Price

All rights reserved

Second edition 2016

About the author

Trevor has been a passionate environmentalist all through his working life. To get a thorough understanding of up-to-date issues, Trevor started off his top flight environmental career with an MSc in Energy Conservation and the Environment, which was quickly followed by a PhD in Environmental Engineering, graduating from the prestigious Cranfield University in the UK. He then spent several years as an Environmental Consultant getting his hands dirty on energy- and environmentally-related projects in the south west of England. This work included developing environmental policies right through to installing renewable energy systems. Having an urge to spread the 'green' message, and building upon his experience in the industry, Trevor then became a Senior University Lecturer. Since 2001 Trevor has been teaching and developing environmentally-related Master degree courses, as well as advising businesses on related topics. He is also the author of over 45 scientific research papers and he currently teaches Environmental Management, as well as other environmentally-flavored subjects to under-graduate and post-graduate university students. As a Senior University Lecturer, Trevor has taught Environmental Management Systems to more than 400 students, leads an MSc in Safety, Health and Environmental Management and has helped organizations become ISO 14001 compliant.

Book summary

This second edition includes updates to reflect the significant changes made to the Environmental Management Systems International Standard ISO 14001 during 2015. The changes made were within the areas of:

- Context of the organization
- Leadership
- Planning
- Support
- Operation
- Performance evaluation
- Improvement

The 2015 update to the EMS Standard 14001 introduced significant changes, i.e.:

- More expectations on senior managers to understand the environmental issues relevant to the organization.
- More emphasis on integrating environmental issues into the strategic management of the organization.
- Requiring organizations to make specific commitments to sustainable development and corporate social responsibility.
- Increasing what an EMS covers, expanding it to include the supply chain and procurement activities.
- Encouraging environmentally-good design.
- Having the ability to show the status of the organization's level of environmental compliance.
- Using performance indicators to monitor improvements.

No matter how big or what your business does, this book will show you how you can design, install and maintain an Environmental Management System that is ISO 14000:2015 compliant, thus enabling you to avoid operating illegally, reducing your organization's environmental footprint and saving money and resources.

This book is aimed at you if you are an Environmental Manager and would like some helpful support in your work. Or perhaps you're a student studying the subject and craving for more knowledge and better understanding? May be you're an experienced employee already working in this important area of business or you're just curious about how the organization you work for can reduce its environmental footprint? Whichever you are, this book gives you all that you need to be able to fully understand what Environmental Management Systems are, what they do and how to build and operate them.

By using this book you will quickly and easily understand how an Environmental Management System can help you reduce the environmental impacts of your business, reduce costs and so enhance and boost your organizations, as well as your own, eco-credentials. Furthermore, in this book are loads of templates that you can easily and quickly customize for your own needs and use within your organization. This will take away all the tedious hassle of starting from scratch, developing an Environmental Management System from nothing, and provides you with a quick route to your own bespoke EMS that's right for your unique business context.

Written by an experienced Environmental Management System designer, developer, auditor, University lecturer and consultant, this book is written in an easy-to-follow way, using a simplified but not patronizing style that is really easy and quick to grasp.

Contents

1   What are Environmental Management Systems? 1

      What does an Environmental Management System aim to achieve? 3

      Changed Environmental Management System terminology 4

      Corporate Social Responsibility 4

2   Integrating Environmental and Quality Management Systems 13

3   Plan phase: Building A Foundation For An Environmental Management System 17

      The context of the organization and defining EMS goals 17

          Context 17

          Goals 18

4   Plan phase: Leadership 21

      Select EMS leaders 23

      Build implementation team 23

      Hold initial meeting 24

      Conduct an Initial Environmental Review 24

      Prepare budget and schedule 25

      Secure resources 26

      Involve employees 26

      Monitor and communicate progress 26

      Ongoing EMS leadership 26

5   Plan phase: Environmental Policy 35

6   Plan phase: Compliance Obligations 41

7   Plan phase: Environmental Aspects and Impacts 45

      Planning actions 49

8	Plan phase: Environmental Objectives	51
9	Plan phase: Environmental Action Plan	55
	Environmental Review for new products, processes and activities	56
10	Do phase: Support	59
	Resources	59
	Competence and awareness	60
	Communication	66
	Identifying which stakeholders to communicate with	67
	Stakeholder roles	68
	How to work with stakeholders	69
	Prioritizing stakeholders	69
	Understanding key stakeholders	72
	Documented Information	76
	Updating and controlling Documented Information	84
11	Do phase: Operation	89
	Operational planning and control	89
	Drafting operational controls	91
	Designate responsibility for maintaining and reviewing operational controls	94
	Develop operational control-related competence	95
	Take Corrective Action when Objectives are not met	96
	Emergency preparedness and response	96
	Getting started	98
12	Check phase: Performance Evaluation	103
	Monitoring, measurement, analysis and evaluation	103
	Monitoring efficiently	104
	Tracking EMS performance	107
	Measuring improved pollution prevention	110
	Calibrating equipment	111

       Energy case study 111
            Space-heating energy monitoring and control 112
       Internal audit 120
       Management Review 129

13 Act phase: Improvement 135
       Non-conformity and Corrective Action 135
       Finding causes of problems 137
       Taking Corrective Action.. 138
       Continual improvement 140

14 Works Cited... 141

15 Index 143

16 Appendix 1: Initial Environmental Review Assessment Checklist 145

17 Appendix 2: Procedure for Identification of Compliance Obligations 151

18 Appendix 3: Procedure for Obtaining Agency Approval 153

19 Appendix 4: Procedure for Environmental Aspects, Objectives, and Action Plans 155

20 Appendix 5: Procedure for Environmental Review for New Purchases, Processes and Products 157

21 Appendix 6: Environmental Impact Assessment Evaluation Checklist 159

22 Appendix 7: Procedure for Environmental Competence 161

23 Appendix 8: Procedure for Communicating With Stakeholders 163

24 Appendix 9: EMS Manual 165

25 Appendix 10: Procedure for Environmental Documented Information 169

26 Appendix 11: Procedure for Document Control 171

27 Appendix 12: Procedure for Contractors and Sub-contractors..........175

28 Appendix 13: Procedure for Emergency Preparedness and Response 185

29 Appendix 14: Procedure for Monitoring, Measurement, Analysis and Evaluation 187

30 Appendix 15: Procedure for Corrective Action 189

31 Appendix 16: Procedure for EMS and Regulatory and other Compliance Obligations Audits 191

32 Appendix 17: Procedure for EMS Management Review....................195

List of Resources

Resource 1 Differences in terminology used in different versions of ISO 14001 5
Resource 2 Steps to help integrate an Environmental Management System with an existing Quality Management System 16
Resource 3 Example of how to define the scope of an EMS 19
Resource 4 Example skills and abilities staff can bring to an EMS project team 29
Resource 5 Questions, the answers to which can help determine the roles and responsibilities of EMS staff 31
Resource 6 A sample description of EMS responsibilities 32
Resource 7 Example EMS Responsibilities 33
Resource 8 Help in developing an Environmental Policy 38
Resource 9 An example Environmental Policy 39
Resource 10 Help in identifying applicable Compliance Obligations 43
Resource 11 Example Environmental Impacts 47
Resource 12 Example Environmental Risk Assessment matrix 49
Resource 13 Example Environmental Objectives and an Action Plan to achieve them 52
Resource 14 Questions, the answers to which can help in planning for and implementing an Environmental Action Plan 57
Resource 15 Questions, the answers to which can help to begin the process of identifying environmental competence requirements. 63
Resource 16 Training Needs Analysis — Environmental Courses 65
Resource 17 Training Needs Analysis — Procedures by area or department 65
Resource 18 Some tips for effective communications 70
Resource 19 Stakeholder Analysis 71
Resource 20 Questions, the answers to which can help you understand stakeholder needs 73
Resource 21 Questions, the answers to which help develop stakeholder communications 74
Resource 22 Communications Program Matrix 75
Resource 23 Record of External Stakeholder Communication 75
Resource 24 Questions, answers to which help develop EMS documentation 78
Resource 25 Questions, answers to which will help you develop information you'll need to document as part of your EMS. 80
Resource 26 Issues to consider when establishing a Documented Information Management Procedure 84
Resource 27 Questions, answers to which will help determine your organization's Documentation Control Procedure 86
Resource 28 Example Master Document List for an EMS Manual 87
Resource 29 Example List of an Organization's Common Areas of Activity and some Associated Operational Controls 91
Resource 30 Questions, answers to which will help in planning EMS Procedures. 92

Resource 31 Worksheet for Determining Which Operations or Activities Require Operational Controls 93
Resource 32 Worksheet to help link Operational Control Procedures to performance indicators. 94
Resource 33 Worksheet for planning environmental training focussed upon an organization's Operational Controls 95
Resource 34 Corrective Action Request 96
Resource 35 Corrective Action Tracking Log 97
Resource 36 Questions, the answers to which help in the development and maintenance of Emergency Preparedness and Response Plans and Procedures 99
Resource 37 Emergency Preparedness and Response Requirements checklist ... 101
Resource 38 Questions, the answers to which will help you determine your organization's EMS monitoring, measurement, analysis and evaluation process 106
Resource 39 EMS Program Measurement Criteria Worksheet 107
Resource 40 Example energy data 115
Resource 41 Help in developing an organization's Audit Procedure 125
Resource 42 Questions, the answers to which can help you to determine your organization's audit Procedure 128
Resource 43 Issues to consider when holding an EMS Management Review 131
Resource 44 EMS Management Review Record 133
Resource 45 Questions, answers to which help develop your organization's Corrective Action Procedure 140
Resource 46 Legal and Compliance Obligations identification 152
Resource 47 Example Index of Environmental Documented Information 170
Resource 48 Example Master documents list 173
Resource 49 Example Contractor Environmental Briefing Statement 177
Resource 50 Contractor Work Method Statement 180

List of Figures

Figure 1 'Plan, Do, Check, Act' Model at the heart of every EMS 1
Figure 2 Links between the Plan, Do, Check, Act model and the ISO 14001 framework 3
Figure 3 Themes within the Environmental Management System model 9
Figure 4 EMS team organization 27
Figure 5 Example EMS Responsibility Matrix 30
Figure 6 Example process map for photocopying a document 47
Figure 7 Elements influencing Environmental Objectives setting 51
Figure 8 Support for an EMS comes from a mix of adequate resources, staff competence and awareness, effective communication and well managed documents 59
Figure 9 Elements comprising an Environmental Communications Plan 67
Figure 10 Power and Interest Stakeholder Matrix 72
Figure 11 How to develop EMS documentation 81
Figure 12 Environmental controls from a life cycle perspective 90
Figure 13 EMS performance evaluation 103
Figure 14 Schematic diagram of heating degree days example 113
Figure 15 Graph of monthly energy consumption data 116
Figure 16 Example energy signature 118
Figure 17 Phases of an Environmental Management System audit 122
Figure 18 Elements considered in the Management Review of an Environmental Management System 130
Figure 19 Management Review outputs 132
Figure 20 Continual improvement is the aim of every EMS 135
Figure 21 Nonconformities and Corrective Actions required 136
Figure 22 Root cause diagram for a milk spill which enabled milk to get into a nearby river, killing some fish 138

Nomenclature

Compliance Obligations	The organization's responsibilities with respect to maintaining legal legitimacy, as well as adherence with other non-mandatory systems and agreements such as Corporate Social Responsibility protocols, organic food standards and ethical trading schemes.
CSR	Corporate Social Responsibility
Cross Functional Team (CFT)	Members of an organization responsible for representing their department in EMS-related work.
Document	Written communication that presents an organization's policy, procedures and other requirements.
EMR	Environmental Management Representative
EMS Coordinator	A staff member who should identify, assign, schedule, provide the necessary support for, and ensure completion of, all tasks relating to the EMS.
EMS	Environmental Management System
Environmental Aspect	An element of an organization's activities, products or services that creates an Environmental Impact.

Environmental Impact	Any change to the environment, whether adverse or beneficial, resulting from an organization's activities, products or services.
Environmental Management Program	Action plans necessary to achieve the organization's objectives.
Environmental Management Representative	A senior manager responsible for the EMS.
Leadership	The act of being the principal responsible person.
Life Cycle	A consideration of the environmental issues of everything that went into the creation, delivery, use and end-of-life of a product or service.
Method Statement	A written statement outlining work to be undertaken and the method(s) for minimizing its Environmental Impacts.
Non-conformance	Discrepancy between an organization's actual EMS activities and the procedures described in its EMS Manual.
Objective	A quantified environmental goal, arising from the Environmental Policy.
Performance Indicator	Measureable criteria that allow an organization to evaluate an EMS Program.

Process Measure	Measured characteristic linked to inputs into an activity, such as the amount of paint used per product.
QMS	Quality Management System
Record	Written evidence established and maintained to track EMS performance.
Risk	Exposure of something to danger, harm or loss.
Significant	Sufficiently important to warrant attention. Within an EMS, elements such as Environmental Aspects and Impacts are categorized as 'significant' if they present relatively high risk to the organization.

1 WHAT ARE ENVIRONMENTAL MANAGEMENT SYSTEMS?

An Environmental Management System, (EMS), is a formalized cycle of planning, implementing, reviewing and improving the processes and actions that an organization undertakes to meet its environmental obligations – see Figure 1.

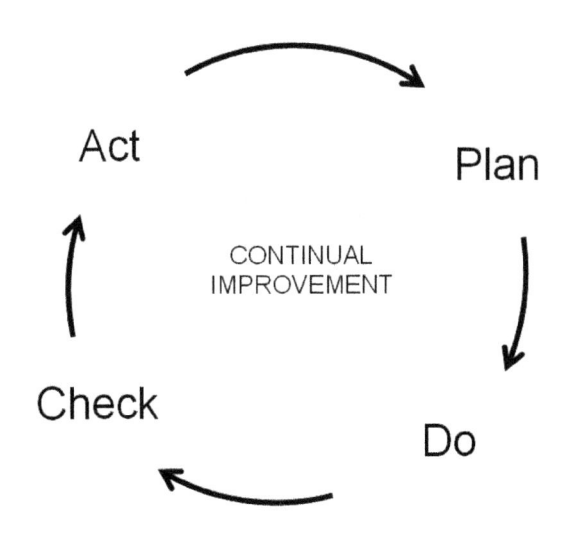

Figure 1 'Plan, Do, Check, Act' Model at the heart of every EMS.

This specifically means that an EMS provides a standardized and certifiable framework that enables organizations to manage and improve the environmental performance of the whole life cycle of their products and/or services whilst ensuring that they comply with environmental legislation and other environmental obligations. In doing so, organizations achieve material and financial savings which ultimately lead to reduced environmental impacts.

An EMS has at its heart a process of continual improvement which is based upon a 'Plan, Do, Check, Act' model and is cyclical in nature. Such a cycle infers that there are always improvements to be made. This also promotes self-regulation as staff are encouraged to continuously look for better ways of working as well as providing added legitimacy to the organization and its operations, in turn reducing or removing business risks and so contributing to long term survival.

The Plan, Do, Check, Act model when applied to an Environmental Management System can be thought of as:

- PLAN – Environmental Objectives and processes are established in order to deliver environmental results that are in line with the organization's stakeholder's needs and expectations as well as the subsequent Environmental Policy.
- DO – processes are implemented as planned.
- CHECK – processes are monitored and measured against the Environmental Policy, the Policy's commitments and the Environmental Objectives and operating criteria. The results are then formally reported.
- ACT – the best actions possible are taken with the aim of continually improving the organizations environmental performance.

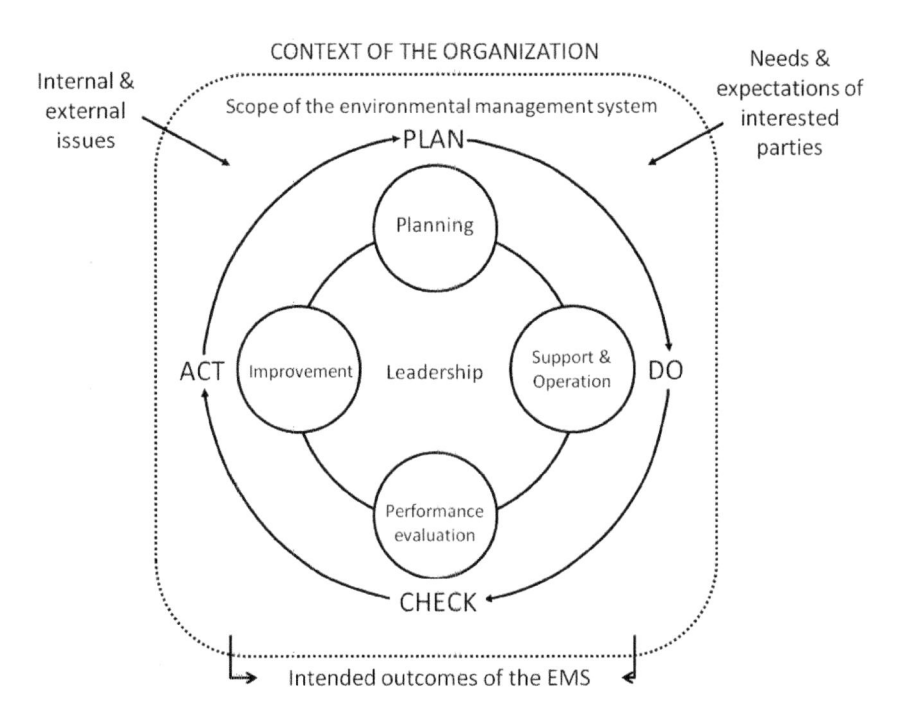

Figure 2 Links between the Plan, Do, Check, Act model and the ISO 14001 framework

The framework for ISO 14001 has therefore been built around the Plan, Do, Check, Act model and so can be incorporated into such as systems approach, as shown in Figure 2 (British Standards Institute, 2015).

WHAT DOES AN ENVIRONMENTAL MANAGEMENT SYSTEM AIM TO ACHIEVE?

As noted in ISO 14001, an EMS provides a structured and formalized way to protect the environment whilst also responding to changing environmental conditions and maintaining balance with socio-economic demands (British Standards Institute, 2015). An EMS can also enable organizations to contribute to sustainable development by:

- Protecting the environment by preventing or mitigating adverse environmental impacts;
- Mitigating the potential adverse effects of environmental conditions on the organization;
- Assisting the organization in the fulfilment of its Compliance Obligations;
- Communicating environmental information to interested parties.
- Enhancing environmental performance;
- Controlling or influencing the way products and services are designed, manufactured, distributed, consumed and disposed of by using a life cycle perspective;
- Achieving financial and operational benefits that can result from implementing environmentally sound alternatives;

CHANGED ENVIRONMENTAL MANAGEMENT SYSTEM TERMINOLOGY

If you have experience with older versions of ISO 14001, you are probably familiar with their terminology. However some of that familiar terminology has been changed or is not used in ISO 14001:2015 as shown in Resource 1.

CORPORATE SOCIAL RESPONSIBILITY

As a minimum, businesses must operate within the law. Most businesses must also generate a profit in order to keep afloat. Businesses also have a duty to provide employment, pay taxes and furnish their shareholders with maximised dividends. Given that these things happen, it could also be argued that businesses also have a moral duty to behave in a responsible way and affect positive change in the world. So businesses not only have a role to play in generating financial benefit, but by following responsible practice and rewarding responsible behaviour, a powerful contract with society can be formed enabling businesses to become engines for positive social change and innovation which is sustainable and long lasting. The term 'Corporate Social Responsibility', (CSR) is used to try to encompass these positive business ideas. CSR therefore encompasses any strategic tool that creates business opportunities, mitigates both internal and external threats to the organisation and its future development, as well as proactively manages reputational risk.

Resource 1 Differences in terminology used in different versions of ISO 14001

ISO 14001:2004	ISO 14001:2015
Legal and other requirements	Compliance Obligations
Documents; records	Documented Information
Management representative	Not used
Preventative action	Not used
Target	Not used
Not used	Leadership
Not used	Risk
Not used	Opportunity
Not used	Environmental conditions
Not used	Life Cycle

CSR is concerned with how organizations respond to answering the changing demands of risk areas in a changing society. Going beyond the economic (i.e. profit making), and legal and regulatory (e.g. health, safety, environmental, stakeholder requirements) business dimensions, CSR is voluntary and brings in line moral and ethical dimensions such as sustainable business, welfare, risk, governance, compliance management and human rights involved in making profit. In essence, CSR is like giving back to the individuals (e.g. employees, investors and geographical neighbors) and wider society who support the organization as well as the environment in which the business operates. Forward thinking organizations will recognize the benefits of being socially responsible and increasingly consider CSR as a natural and normal way of doing business. Less clued-up organizations not only miss such opportunities, they might be attracted by, or at least persuaded somehow to follow, the less-than-positive path to non-ethical business practices (mistreating staff and subcontractors and polluting for example) that morally reprehensible businesses follow.

Corporate social responsibility therefore can encompass a wide range of issues: from the minutiae of running the business, to issues of global significance. What the priorities are is really down to the size of the business, its scope, its product and services, its reputation, its track record, its age and its current and historical corporate record. For example, the issues of relevance to a company such as Google, with its international reach are very different to the issues of relevance to a florist operating in only one town.

Not only is the reality of an organization's performance on corporate social responsibility important to its future success but its perceived CSR performance is also vital. Therefore the wise and good management of Corporate Social Responsibility within an organization can influence competitive advantage; reputation; ability to attract and keep staff and customers; the maintenance of employee's morale, commitment and productivity; the view of investors and the organization's relationship with subcontractors, suppliers, government agencies, the media and the community within which it operates. CSR therefore is all about how organizations interact with their stakeholders whilst undertaking their day-to-day business operations. It is unavoidably linked to sustainable development and so obliges organizations to make decisions based on financial/economic factors, e.g. financial profits, Return on Investments and shareholder dividend payments, but also on the wider environmental and social consequences of their activities. It is clear therefore that Corporate Social Responsibility does not focus solely upon social issues. Comprehensive Corporate Social Responsibility encompasses issues that the organization can have some influence over and can affect. Usually this means issues with respect to the environmental impacts of the business, as well as the quality of its products/services and how people who are linked to the business are treated. Environmental Management Systems therefore play a key role in boosting an organization's CSR credentials especially now that Environmental Management Systems accredited to ISO 14001 require organizations to consider the all encompassing environmental impacts of the products they design and make, as well as the services they provide. Therefore an assessment of the 'life cycle' of these things, from their design right through to the disposal of their constituent parts is required.

To improve the management of their environmental impacts, organizations should focus not only upon what types of issues arise but also on <u>why</u> they happen. Over time the identification and correction of such issues will lead to better environmental, and overall, organizational performance.

An EMS is also usually accredited to a standard such as ISO 14001 and so provides a recognizable way to show stakeholders that the organization is serious about its environmental credentials. An EMS doesn't only result in such enhanced environmental performance - other positive side-effects of such a System also include cost savings, improved legislative compliance, along with other risk and liability reductions. An EMS can also aid the perception stakeholders have of the organization, boosting positivity and so aiding competitive advantage.

To ensure successful implementation and maintenance of an Environmental Management System senior managers need to be committed to the EMS project as there will be some associated costs such as staff time when they are working on EMS related tasks and the possibility of hiring outside experts to help solve specific challenges. Applying the 'Plan, Do, Check, Act' principles, as well as providing appropriate resources are the job of senior managers. The senior management team must also initiate and sustain the EMS effort. This they can achieve by communicating to all employees the importance of making the environment an organizational priority, integrating environmental management throughout the organization and approaching problems with the view that such problems are really positive opportunities to improve how their organization works. There will also need to be a focus upon continual improvement and so recognizing that problems will occur as unfortunately no organization is perfect.

An effective EMS must also be dynamic to allow the organization to adapt to a quickly changing environment. Therefore the EMS should be as flexible and simple as possible. This in turn enables the EMS to be easily understandable by the people who must implement it – especially managers and other employees. The EMS should also be compatible with the culture of the organization. For some organizations this involves a choice between tailoring the EMS to the organization's culture or changing the culture to be compatible with the EMS approach. The latter approach can be quite difficult and is usually a longer-term process!

The awareness and involvement of employees is another key to a successful EMS. As an EMS is designed and implemented, challenging roadblocks are often encountered. Some may view an EMS as another layer of bureaucracy or extra expense imposed upon staff. There may also be resistance to change or fear of new responsibilities and extra workload. To overcome such possible challenges, ensuring that everyone understands why the organization needs an effective EMS, what their role will be and how an EMS will help control the negative, and enhance the positive, environmental impacts in a cost-effective way can all help. Such well thought-out employee involvement also helps to demonstrate the organization's commitment to the environment and helps to ensure that the EMS is realistic, practical and that it actually adds value.

Building the EMS upon the 'Plan, Do, Check, Act' Model also ensures that environmental matters are systematically identified, controlled and monitored. Using such an approach also helps ensure that performance of the EMS improves over time.

At a strategic level an EMS will usually have the six main themes shown in Figure 3 of Context Setting; Leadership; Planning; Support; Performance Evaluation; and Improvement. To develop an EMS from scratch staff within the organization need to start by thinking about the context in which the organization is situated. Also by asking 'Why?' things that have an environmental consequence are the way they are helps you gain a better understanding of the organization and greatly aids subsequent EMS development.

Improvement
- Nonconformity & corrective action
- Continual improvement

Organizational context START
- Understand the organization & its context; the needs & expectations of interested parties
- Determine scope of EMS

Performance evaluation
- Monitoring, measurement, analysis & evaluation
- Evaluation of compliance
- Internal audit programme
- Management review

Leadership
- Show leadership
- Environmental policy
- Organizational roles, responsibilities & authorities

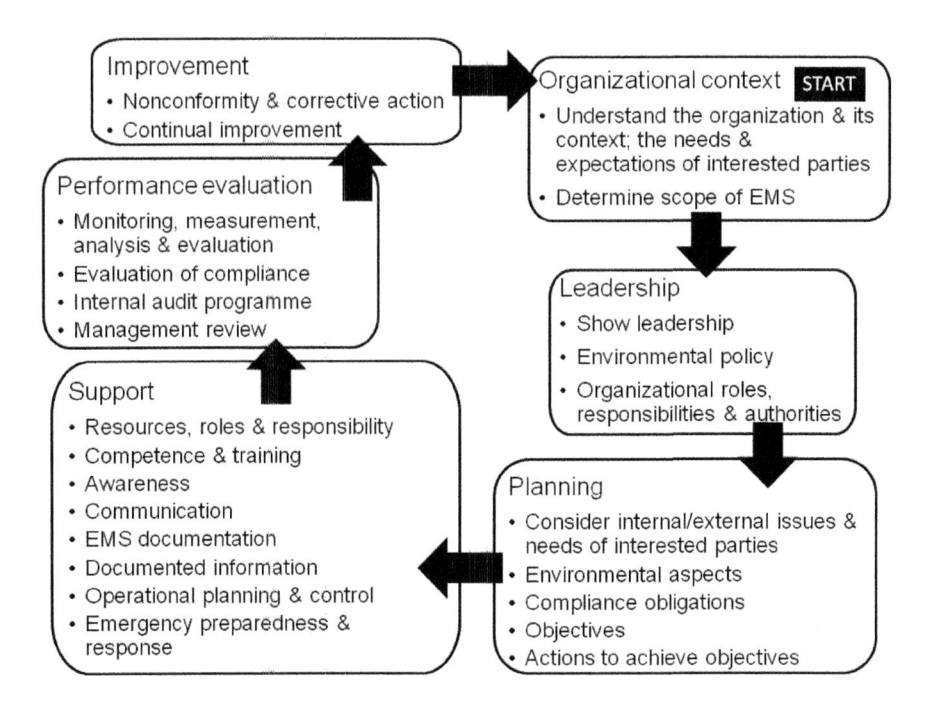

Support
- Resources, roles & responsibility
- Competence & training
- Awareness
- Communication
- EMS documentation
- Documented information
- Operational planning & control
- Emergency preparedness & response

Planning
- Consider internal/external issues & needs of interested parties
- Environmental aspects
- Compliance obligations
- Objectives
- Actions to achieve objectives

Figure 3 Themes within the Environmental Management System model

Within the six themes shown in Figure 3, there are other specific elements to an EMS, these being:

- **Context of the organization** – determine external and internal factors that impact upon the organization's ability to achieve the planned EMS outcomes. These should include those environmental factors being affected by the organization as well as those affecting the organization.
- **Structure and responsibility** – establish roles and responsibilities for environmental management and provide appropriate resources.
- **Environmental Policy** – develop a statement of the organization's commitment to protecting the environment. Use this Policy as a framework for planning and action.
- **Compliance Obligations** – identify and ensure access to relevant laws and regulations, as well as other requirements to which the organization adheres.
- **Environmental Aspects** – identify environmental attributes of the organization's products, activities and services from a lifecycle perspective. Determine those that could have Significant Environmental Impacts during normal, abnormal and emergency situations.
- **Environmental Objectives** – establish Environmental Objectives for your organization in line with the Environmental Policy, Environmental Impacts, the views of interested parties and any other relevant factors.
- **Environmental Management Program** – plan actions to achieve the Environmental Objectives considering the identified risks and opportunities.
- **Competence and awareness** – ensure that employees are trained and are competent in carrying out their environmental responsibilities.
- **Communication** – establish processes for communications on environmental management issues to occur within, and out from, the organization. Plan what, when, how and with whom communications are made.
- **Documented Information** – maintain information on the organization's EMS and related documents.

- **Document control** – ensure effective management of Procedures and other information; that Documented Information is in the appropriate format and media and that it is adequately protected.
- **Operational planning and control** – identify, plan and manage the operations and activities in line with the Environmental Policy and Objectives.
- **Emergency preparedness and response** – identify possible emergencies and develop procedures for preventing and responding to them.
- **Monitoring, measurement, analysis and evaluation** – monitor key activities and evaluate performance using appropriate indicators.
- **Evaluation of compliance** – know and understand the organization's level of compliance.
- **EMS audits** – use competent staff to check and verify that the EMS is operating properly.
- **Management Review** – periodically review the EMS with the intention of continually improving and to find ways to better integrate the EMS with other business processes.
- **Non-conformity and Corrective Action** – consider if similar nonconformities exist or could potentially happen and put in place actions to correct problems.
- **Continual improvement** – create an ethos, organizational structure and systems that ensure that environmental performance will be continually improved.

2   INTEGRATING ENVIRONMENTAL AND QUALITY MANAGEMENT SYSTEMS

If the organization already has a Quality Management System there will be significant synergy between the requirements of the Quality and the Environmental Management Systems. Any Health and Safety Program can also play a significant part in an EMS as it reflects how the organization handles human health concerns. In many areas health and safety and environmental requirements are similar and so some requirements may be addressed concurrently. Therefore some organizations find that integrating health and safety and EMS efforts can achieve improved compliance and cost savings. In fact integrating management systems that have some similar structures has become an increasingly popular approach and is encouraged by the International Organization for Standardization by the use of 'Annex SL' which is a similar 'high level structure' used across and within similar standards such as ISO 14001 and its Quality and Health and Safety counterparts. Organizations that integrate their Environmental, Quality and Health and Safety Management Systems can realize significant benefits, such as:

- Streamlined operations.
- Better decision-making.
- Simplified employee training.
- Efficient use of resources.
- Reductions in audit costs.

The two most common models for Quality Management Systems and Environmental Management Systems are ISO 9001 and ISO 14001 respectively – both of which share many common elements. This is not surprising as ISO 9001 was one of the source documents used by the developers of ISO 14001. The two standards are therefore relatively easily compatible. Organizations that choose to implement both standards generally find that they can use many common processes as in general the elements of a QMS and EMS can be categorized as essentially the same, similar or unique, viz:

- **Elements that are essentially the same:** Leadership, Training, Awareness and Competence; Documented Information Control; Non-conformance and Corrective Action; and Calibration (which is part of Monitoring and Measurement).
- **Elements that are similar:** Stakeholder evaluation; Policy; Structure and Responsibility; Documented Information; Operational Control; Monitoring and Measurement; Audits and Management Review.
- **Elements that are unique to EMS:** Environmental Aspects; Compliance Obligations; Objectives; Environmental Management Program; Communications and Emergency Preparedness and Response; and Life Cycle Assessment.

System elements in both the *'essentially the same'* and *'similar'* categories can often be addressed by common or parallel Procedures although some customization may be needed to address the differing overall purposes of each system. Unique elements are typically dealt with in separate EMS or QMS procedures. The System parts that can be easily integrated are those that cover leadership, Documented Information control and management, corrective action, training, and management review.

While an EMS can be readily integrated with an existing QMS the overall purposes of these two Systems must be kept in mind. A QMS is intended primarily to ensure that an organization satisfies its customers by assuring the quality of its products. An EMS however also has a broader context about the relationship between the organization and the environment in which it operates. An EMS also often concerns itself with a broader range of stakeholders, such as neighboring communities, customers and regulatory agencies and should also consider the holistic environmental impacts of the business activities from their conception through to conclusion.

System integration can also have environmental benefits. By linking environmental management more closely with the day-to-day planning and operation of the organization, some organizations have been able to raise the visibility of environmental management as an important organizational issue. In addition, these organizations have been able to enhance their abilities to address environmental issues when making modifications to products or processes for quality purposes. This has in turn led to more positive environmental performance.

Organizations that have a QMS in place generally are better off when implementing an EMS for several reasons. Firstly, employees are typically already familiar with Management System concepts and are already also involved in making the System work. Secondly, many of the processes needed for the EMS might already be in place. Finally, and perhaps most importantly, senior managers have become committed to the use of Management Systems to achieve organizational goals. For organizations that have an existing QMS and wish to integrate an EMS with it, some useful steps to take are shown in Resource 2.

Resource 2 Steps to help integrate an Environmental Management System with an existing Quality Management System

Understand the existing Quality Management System, its effectiveness and how staff perceive the System.

Is the existing Quality Management System documentation clear and workable? Do employees believe that the System is helping the organization achieve desired results?

Establish a Cross Functional Team to determine the optimal approach to System integration.

Manage resistance to change. Some employees and managers may be reluctant to change a System with which they are already familiar or in which they have important roles.

Understand how the Quality Management System and Environmental Management System differ. While there are many common Management System elements, there are elements of each System that are unique. Such differences must be acknowledged and accommodated within the integrated Management System.

Modify System documentation. Keep Procedures simple and clear. Review proposed changes with affected staff.

Consider whether to integrate Procedures or keep them separate on a Procedure-by-Procedure basis. While integration can reduce the total number of Procedures or work instructions, in some cases it can confuse the overall purpose of such Procedures.

Train staff on the integrated System once its documentation has been prepared.

3   PLAN PHASE: BUILDING A FOUNDATION FOR AN ENVIRONMENTAL MANAGEMENT SYSTEM

The following are the key steps for ensuring that the development and implementation of an Environmental Management Systems starts well.

THE CONTEXT OF THE ORGANIZATION AND DEFINING EMS GOALS

CONTEXT

How exactly this part of the EMS is addressed by staff within organizations is open to interpretation. At a minimum this could be addressed simply by discussing issues such as geographical location, describing suppliers and describing sub-contractors and outsourcing. A far better and more comprehensive approach however would be to ask questions about the organization that start with 'Why?' By moving past the simple need for financial gain, finding answers to questions such as why . . .

- . . .   Does the organization exist?
- . . .   Do we use these items?
- . . .   Do we use these suppliers, processes, machines, sub-contractors, products and materials?

. . . can help the easier development of Environmental Policy, Objectives and subsequent Action Plans.

It is a requirement that all (external and internal) issues that affect the organization's ability to achieve the intended outcomes of its EMS be determined. This will include considering the needs and expectations of all stakeholders.

Goals

Decide why you are pursuing the development of an EMS. Are you trying to improve your organization's environmental performance? For example, reducing risk associated with regulatory non-compliance or increasingly stringent pollution prevention? Are you trying to promote more staff involvement in environmental issues throughout the organization? As you design and implement the EMS, question how the task in hand is going to help you achieve your Environmental Objectives? This is also a good time to define the scope of your EMS - i.e. what exactly is the 'organization' that the EMS will cover? Does it have only one or multiple locations? Should you pilot-test the EMS at one location and then implement the System at other locations later?

To define the scope of your EMS, define boundaries around your organization's activities and determine the areas that staff within your organization can control and over which they have influence. You should consider items such as external and internal issues, its environmental Compliance Obligations, as well as the range, and level, of authority it has to determine how the Environmental Policy is implemented as well as do staff have sufficient power to allocate appropriate resources? At this stage it is also wise to consider the organization's authority and ability to exercise control and influence throughout the entire life cycle of its products and services. This should include design choices right through to the ultimate end of the product and/or service.

An example of how to define the scope of an EMS is shown in Resource 3.

For initial development of its EMS you may find that it is most effective to limit the scope of the EMS to any activities that occur within the organization's physical property or that occur on adjacent property as a direct result of the organizations operations. For example, wastewater discharges or storm water run-off. However, for accreditation to ISO 14001 you will also need to expand the scope of the EMS to include post consumer disposal and other life-cycle considerations. Temporary activities such as construction sites and transportation should also be covered by the EMS if the organization has some level of control over them.

Resource 3 Example of how to define the scope of an EMS

Scope of ABC Organization's EMS

The ABC Company has ship repair facilities in California, Louisiana and Virginia. The Company is committed to improving environmental performance through the use of innovative techniques such as EMS, which it is implementing through a phased, organization-by-organization approach. Thus, while the Company's EMS currently covers only its New Orleans, Louisiana, organization it has plans to address its other facilities through EMSs over time.

The EMS for ABC Company's New Orleans organization includes all on-site operations that support ship repair and related operations (e.g., equipment maintenance, ship transport and storage, shipyard maintenance, administrative functions, and contractors working on the property). The EMS also addresses emissions and discharges regulated through environmental permits and other Compliance Obligations. However, the EMS includes only those Environmental Aspects over which the organization has control or influence. For example, the EMS addresses waste disposal even though the organization is not the final waste disposal site. Rather, the organization will influence the safe disposition of wastes through research and periodic audits of its waste transport and disposal contractors. Also, the sustainability of the materials, products and services used is regularly reviewed with respect to Corporate Social Responsibility performance indicators. In this way ABC Company supports environmental enhancements linked to its EMS.

4   PLAN PHASE: LEADERSHIP

It is a requirement of an EMS that the organization's senior management demonstrate leadership of, as well as their commitment to, the organization's EMS. Such leadership has three elements:

- Senior management leadership and commitment.
- Support for the Environmental Policy.
- Clearly communicated organizational roles, responsibilities and authorities.

One of the most crucial steps in the EMS planning process is gaining senior managers' commitment to leading EMS development and the System's ongoing implementation. In order to be able to give their support such managers usually want to first understand the benefits of an EMS, as well as the costs of what it will take to put in place. This you can achieve by explaining the strengths and limitations of your organization's current approach and how those limitations can affect the organization's financial and operational performance. Then explain how an EMS can help address these limitations. Once committed to an EMS, managers have a significant role in ensuring that the goals for the EMS are clear, consistent and aligned to other organizational goals and priorities. Once such goals have been agreed the organization's senior managers' commitment to the EMS should be regularly communicated across the organization. Such commitment to the Environmental Management System comes in the form of:

- Being accountable for the EMS.
- Establishing the Environmental Policy and Objectives and ensuring that they align with the organization's context and strategic direction.
- Integrating EMS requirements into the organization's day-to-day business processes.

- Ensuring adequate resources for the EMS are available.
- Communicating the importance of the EMS and conforming to its requirements.
- Ensuring the EMS achieves its intended outcomes.
- Supporting people to contribute to the EMS.
- Promoting continual improvement.
- Supporting all relevant managers to demonstrate their leadership with respect to their areas of responsibility.

SELECT EMS LEADERS

Small organization's may only have a single EMS 'champion', but larger ones will usually have two levels of EMS leadership. An Environmental Management Representative, (EMR) should be chosen from the organization's senior management team to be responsible for ensuring that all tasks relating to the EMS are identified and completed in a timely manner. The EMR is responsible for reporting periodically to the senior management group on the progress and results of the EMS. An EMS Coordinator is also required who has time to commit to the EMS design, building and maintenance processes because his or her responsibility will be to work closely with the EMR and with the Cross Functional Team, (CFT) to identify, assign, schedule, provide the necessary support for, and ensure the completion of, all tasks relating to the EMS.

BUILD IMPLEMENTATION TEAM

A Cross Functional Team with representatives from the appropriate management functions, such as engineering, finance, human resources, production and/or services should be established. Such a team can be useful to help identify and assess environmental issues, opportunities for improvements and existing processes that can be beneficially harnessed by an EMS. Such a team helps ensure that the developed EMS procedures are practical and effective and can build commitment to and 'ownership' of the EMS. Where appropriate and where they can add valuable input consider including contractors, suppliers or other external parties as part of the CFT. The CFT will need to meet regularly, especially in the early stages of your EMS efforts.

HOLD INITIAL MEETING

Once the Cross Functional Team has been selected, hold an initial meeting to discuss the organization's environmental goals and reasons for implementing the EMS, what actions need to be taken and the roles and responsibilities of each team member. If possible get senior managers to describe their commitment to the EMS at this meeting to underline their resolve to the EMS and to also set the scene for forthcoming EMS work. This initial meeting is also a good opportunity to provide some EMS training for CFT members. Follow this meeting with a communication to all other employees letting them know what's happened at the meeting and future planned actions.

CONDUCT AN INITIAL ENVIRONMENTAL REVIEW

The next step is for the CFT to conduct a gap analysis of the organization's current levels of compliance and other environmental systems (if they exist) and to compare these against the criteria for the EMS. This will be an evaluation of, for example, the organization's current structure, Procedures, Policies, Environmental Impacts and Training Programs. Determine which parts of the current EMS are in good shape and which need additional work. Although such gap analysis is important, it can be counter-productive if you only focus on what it is the organization is missing. It is also important to recognize what the organization is already doing and to evaluate ways to improve and build on existing programs and activities. Some organizations may find that they already perform many of the suggested activities. This is good as there is no need to rebuild a program from scratch. Looking outside the environmental arena at this stage can also provide inspiration. For example an area such as a Quality Management System may not be environmentally-focused but may help with developing the EMS. If an activity that is already performing well and helps important business activities run smoothly, it can probably help as part of an Environmental Management System as well. An Initial Environmental Review is therefore designed to answer the following questions:

- How well are the organization and its Environmental Programs performing?
- Has the organization defined the environmental goals it hopes to achieve?
- What are the gaps between any existing Programs and the criteria for an EMS?
- What, if any, existing Programs and activities can serve as the best foundation for improved environmental performance?

Building on existing Programs becomes even more important when organizations are faced with diminishing resources and are being asked to 'do more with less.' Luckily through careful analysis, organizations will probably find ways to address some EMS elements at little or no cost. For example, developing a Policy on environmental protection does not require large investments in personnel or equipment, yet it can enhance organization-wide visibility of environmental issues and can then have significant positive impact.

Appendix 1: Initial Environmental Review Assessment Checklist provides a useful resource that can be used by staff in any organization to assess the organization's current programs and any specific operational needs required in the development of an EMS.

PREPARE BUDGET AND SCHEDULE

Once the Initial Environmental Review has been completed you can prepare an Implementation Plan with a clear budget and schedule. The Plan should identify what key actions are needed, who will be responsible for completing such actions, what resources are needed and when the actions will be completed. Keep the Plan flexible but set some environmental performance improvement goals. Think about how to maintain project focus and momentum over time. Look for possible early successes that can help build such momentum and reinforce the benefits to staff of the EMS and why it should continue.

Secure resources

The Plan and budget should be reviewed and approved by the organization's senior managers. In some cases there may be outside funding or other types of assistance available. Sometimes a trade association or local government authority can help.

Involve employees

Employees are a great source of knowledge not only about environmental, health and safety issues related to their work areas but also about the effectiveness of current processes and procedures. They can also provide valuable help the EMS project team in drafting new and improved procedures. Ownership of the EMS will therefore be enhanced by creating meaningful employee involvement in this part of the EMS development process making such development work easier and more effective.

Monitor and communicate progress

As the EMS is built, regularly monitor progress against the Implementation Plan and communicate this progress within the organization. Also be sure to communicate the accomplishments that have been made and describe what is going to happen next. This will help keep people informed and working towards the same objective. Build on small successes such as publicising your first Environmental Policy, reductions in scrapped work or cuts in utility bills. Remember to also keep senior managers informed and engaged, especially if additional resources might be needed in the future.

Ongoing EMS leadership

One of the first tasks of EMS planning is to establish the roles and responsibilities associated with EMS leadership and technical support. The previous *'Select EMS Leaders'* section of this book provides guidance for establishing such roles and responsibilities during the EMS planning and budgeting process. This section meanwhile addresses the closely related task of creating an ongoing structure that ensures the organization is equipped with sufficient personnel and other resources to meet its Environmental Objectives and ensure the organization's Compliance Obligations are met.

It is important to designate as soon as possible after starting the EMS project, the Environmental Management Representative (EMR), the EMS Coordinator and the Cross Functional Team (CFT), all of whom will play a role in developing and promoting the EMS. Figure 4 shows suggestion of the EMS team members. If the organization is small, these roles could be given to the same person. Even so, it is still important to designate who will be responsible for all the various EMS-related activities.

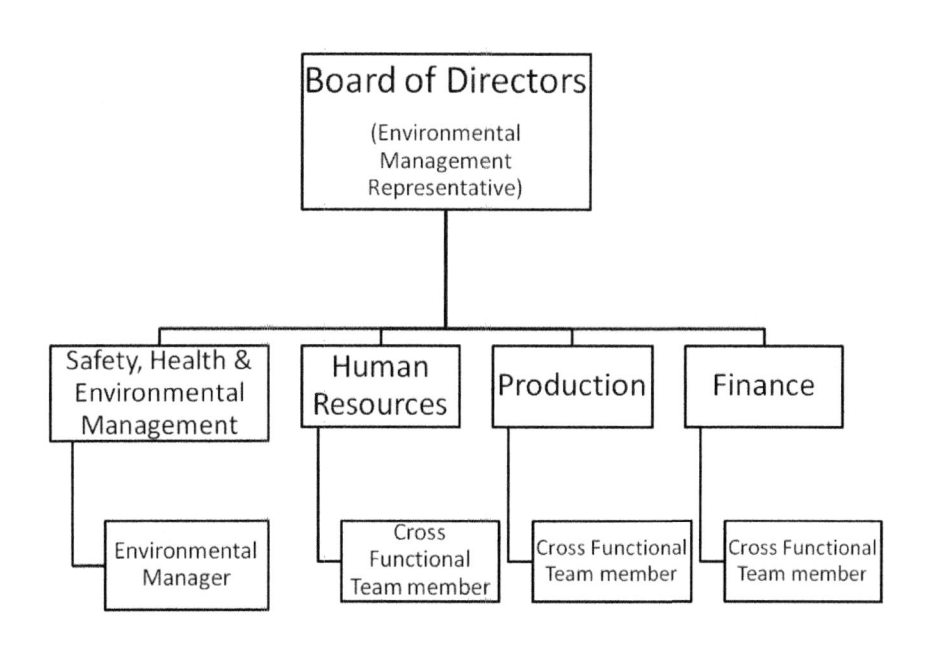

Figure 4 EMS team organization

The EMR is the member of the organization's senior management team who is responsible for the functioning of the EMS. The EMR ensures that all tasks relating to the EMS are identified and completed in a timely manner. The EMR is also responsible for reporting periodically to other senior managers on the progress and results of the EMS.

The EMS Coordinator is responsible for identifying, assigning, scheduling, providing the necessary support for, and ensuring completion of, all EMS-related tasks. The EMS Coordinator works closely with the EMR and the CFT. The EMS Coordinator is also responsible for maintaining the EMS Manual, under the leadership of the EMR. It is possible for the functions of EMS Coordinator and EMR to be performed by the same person. Indeed, and especially in smaller organizations, this will be a necessity in order to keep costs down.

The CFT includes members of the organization who are responsible for representing their area or department in several facets of the EMS, such as identifying Environmental Aspects, determining the significance of those Aspects, setting Environmental Objectives, implementing Environmental Management Programs, reviewing and tracking EMS internal audits results and serving as a source of environmental information. The CFT should meet regularly to ensure that the EMS is running smoothly and that planned, and indeed unplanned remedial actions are taken in a timely manner.

In assigning EMS responsibilities and creating the EMS team it is crucial to explore the range of job functions and skills that make up the organization, and select from that broad spectrum of people who can then dedicate themselves and their skills to the EMS tasks. You can then consider the organization's structure as a list of job functions and skills which can be tapped into to support your EMS planning and implementation efforts. Some suggestions of expertise often found within different parts of organizations are shown in Resource 4.

Resource 4 Example skills and abilities staff can bring to an EMS project team

Staff function	Expertise	How they can help
Finance	Systems for tracking costs of operations and evaluating cost and benefits of new projects	Track data on environmental-related costs (such as resource, material and energy costs, waste disposal costs); prepare budgets for Environmental Management Programs; evaluate economic feasibility of environmental projects.
Environmental	Systems for complying with environmental obligations and management of Documented Information	Establishing and maintaining the EMS.
Facilities Engineering	Management of Environmental Aspects of new construction and installation of equipment	Considering Environmental Impacts of new or modified products and processes; identifying pollution prevention opportunities.
Maintenance	Management of Environmental Aspects of equipment maintenance	Implementing preventive maintenance program for key equipment; supporting identification of Environmental Aspects.

Figure 5 shows an example Responsibility Matrix which identifies some example EMS activities and how they might apply to the various personnel that perform these and other functions within the organization. The lead staff shown in Figure 5 would be good to have as members of the EMS Cross Functional Team.

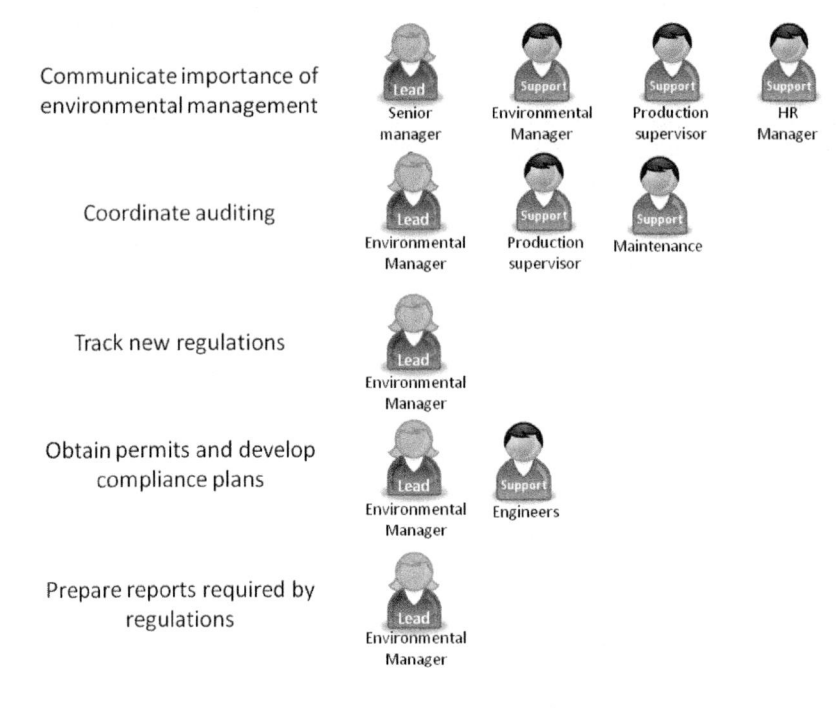

Task				
Communicate importance of environmental management	Senior manager (Lead)	Environmental Manager (Support)	Production supervisor (Support)	HR Manager (Support)
Coordinate auditing	Environmental Manager (Lead)	Production supervisor (Support)	Maintenance (Support)	
Track new regulations	Environmental Manager (Lead)			
Obtain permits and develop compliance plans	Environmental Manager (Lead)	Engineers (Support)		
Prepare reports required by regulations	Environmental Manager (Lead)			

Figure 5 Example EMS Responsibility Matrix

An organization chart showing EMS-related staff and their responsibilities should be included in the EMS Manual – see Figure 4 for an example of this. Resource 5 provides some questions, the answers to which can help you determine the roles and responsibilities of EMS staff.

> *Resource 5 Questions, the answers to which can help determine the roles and responsibilities of EMS staff*
>
> *How do we define roles, responsibilities and authorities for environmental management now? Is this process effective?*
>
> *Who is, or should be, our Environmental Management Representative?*
>
> *Does the Environmental Management Representative have the necessary authority to carry out the responsibilities of this job?*
>
> *Are our key roles and responsibilities for environmental management documented in some way? If so, how?*
>
> *How are EMS roles and responsibilities communicated within the organization?*
>
> *How do we ensure that adequate resources have been allocated for environmental management?*
>
> *How is this environmental management integrated with our overall budgeting process?*
>
> *How is environmental expenditure tracked?*
>
> *How is information kept up-to-date?*

An example description of the environmentally-related responsibilities of staff is provided in Resource 6.

Resource 6 A sample description of EMS responsibilities

[Organization's Name] *needs to establish an EMS Team made up of an Environmental Management Representative, an EMS Coordinator and a Cross Functional Team. The responsibilities of each are:*

Environmental Management Representative. The Environmental Management Representative is the member of **[Organization's Name]'s** *senior management responsible for the functioning of the EMS. It is his or her job to ensure that all tasks relating to the EMS are identified and completed in a timely manner. He or she is also responsible for reporting periodically to other senior management on the progress and results of the EMS.*

EMS Coordinator. The EMS Coordinator's should identify, assign, schedule, provide the necessary support for, and ensure completion of, all tasks relating to the EMS. The EMS Coordinator is also responsible for maintaining the EMS Manual, under the leadership of the Environmental Management Representative.

Cross Functional Team. The Cross Functional Team is made up of staff responsible for representing their area in the EMS, such as establishing Environmental Aspects, determining Significant Aspects, setting Objectives, implementing Environmental Management Programs, reviewing and tracking EMS internal audits results.

Documented Information: The EMS Coordinator maintains a list of the EMRs, the EMS coordinator and Cross Functional Team members. A letter issued by senior managers that assigns the current Environmental Management Representatives and his or her responsibilities is maintained as part of the organization's EMS Manual and is attached to the EMS Responsibilities Data Sheet – see Resource 7.

Such a description is necessary to ensure staff have a clear understanding of their environmental roles, the responsibilities that go with such a role and what other people can then expect of the person undertaking that function.

Resource 7 provides an example data sheet which can be used to keep track of who the EMS CFT membership is along with their individual responsibilities.

Resource 7 Example EMS Responsibilities

EMS function	Name	Responsibilities	Date appointed
Environmental Management Representative			
EMS co-coordinator			
Cross Functional Team member 1			
Cross Functional Team member 2			

The efforts of the EMS Team (i.e. the EMR, the EMS Coordinator and the CFT) will be crucial to the effective implementation and the long-term success of the organization's EMS. In-depth training for the EMS Team on how to plan and implement an EMS and integrate it with existing organization operations is required at this early stage so that the team can be effective in their EMS work. After the EMS implementation training has been completed, the CFT can move onto other activities such as drafting an Environmental Policy, reviewing environmental Compliance Obligations and identifying Environmental Aspects.

5   PLAN PHASE: ENVIRONMENTAL POLICY

Once the organization has its EMS team trained and in place, the next step in developing an EMS is to create a working draft of the organization's Environmental Policy. Such a Policy should fit within the organization's context and the needs and expectations of its stakeholders, as well as being relevant and being situated within the scope of its EMS.

An Environmental Policy contains a statement of organizational commitment to the environment and is a framework for all subsequent environmental action planning. An Environmental Policy is more than just the senior management's declaration of commitment to improved environmental performance: it is also the crucial foundation for the organization's EMS, providing a unifying vision of the environmental issues of concern to the key organizational stakeholders. The Environmental Policy is vital in showing the world that there is commitment from the senior decision makers of the organization to reduce the organization's negative environmental impacts and that the environmental concerns of the important stakeholders have been taken into consideration. It is therefore critical that everyone in the organization understands the Policy, what it means for them, what is expected of them and that the organization and its staff are now committed to continual environmental improvement.

The Environmental Policy should set out the organization's overall commitment to a more sustainable environment as well as containing an assessment of the entire life cycle of what it does. Examples of some of the commitments that should be stated in the EMS Policy are:

- Adherence to the organization's Compliance Obligations.
- Pollution prevention.

- Continuous improvement of the organization's environmental performance including areas not subject to regulations and those that address the needs and expectations of its stakeholders.
- Sharing information about environmental performance and the operation of the EMS with the organization's stakeholders.

An Environmental Policy usually exists - even if it's not written down. For example the organisation is, hopefully, committed to complying with the law and avoiding major environmental problems. If embarking on a completely new EMS it is helpful and saves some work if you can document existing environmentally-relevant commitments and goals. This can be a useful starting point when developing an Environmental Policy and one which staff can usually easily accept and work towards. The Environmental Policy should always relate to the products, services and supporting activities that are relevant to the organization, including an assessment of the life cycle of its operations, services and/or products. The Policy should also be kept as simple and understandable as possible – after all, all staff will need to be able to comprehend the Policy. The results of later stages of EMS development, such as undertaking an Environmental Aspects analysis, should be considered before finalising the Environmental Policy as unknown issues could be unearthed at these latter stages.

The Environmental Policy should also be explicit enough to be audited as the Environmental Policy is used to provide the framework for forming subsequent Environmental Objectives. Therefore it is important to avoid vague statements such as:

'We are committed to excellence and leadership in protecting the environment'

Measuring the success of such a statement will prove to be difficult. Of much more value would be a specific statement of how the Objective will be achieved and how achievement could be measured. For example:

> 'By reducing the use of fossil fuels by switching energy supplies to 100% renewable energy within the next 12 months.'

The process of developing an Environmental Policy can be helped by answering the questions shown in Resource 8.

In general an Environmental Policy should contain a statement of commitment to continuous improvement, along with recognition of compliance with relevant obligations – especially environmental legislation as a minimum level of performance. Following this, mention should be made of the education, training and competence of employees in environmental issues and the environmental effects of their activities as well as the monitoring of progress and review of environmental performance on a regular (usually annual) basis. An example Environmental Policy is shown in Resource 9 which can be customized and used as a starting point in developing a Policy specific to any organization.

Resource 8 Help in developing an Environmental Policy

Do we have an existing Environmental Policy?

How was the Policy developed?

When was the Policy last reviewed?

Does the Policy reflect key commitments, for example, compliance, prevention of pollution and continual improvement?

What other commitments should the Policy contain?

How does the Policy take into account the environmental attributes throughout the life cycle of the organization's activities, products and services?

How would staff demonstrate conformance to the Policy?

How is the Policy communicated to employees?

Do employees understand the critical elements of the Policy? How do we know?

What feedback has been received on the Policy from employees, contractors or other interested parties?

What happens when feedback is received about the Policy?

How is the Policy made available to external parties? Is this process effective?

Our next step on Environmental Policy is to...

Resource 9 An example Environmental Policy

*It is the Policy of **[Organization's Name]** to conduct its operations in a manner that is environmentally responsible and befitting of a good corporate neighbor and citizen. In accordance with this Policy, **[Organization's Name]** complies with all environmental laws and manages all parts of its business in a way that minimizes the impact of its operations on the environment. To further this Policy, **[Organization's Name]** shall:*

Wherever its influence can be applied seek to enhance the environmental performance throughout the life cycle of its products, services and systems.

Comply with applicable environmental laws and regulations and voluntary commitments to which the organization and its stakeholders subscribe.

Eliminate or reduce to the minimum practical extent the release of contaminants into the environment, first through pollution prevention, then recycling, and finally through treatment and control technologies.

Effectively communicate with its stakeholders such as staff, suppliers, regulators and customers, as well as the surrounding community, about its EMS performance.

Periodically review and demonstrate continuous improvement in the organization's environmental performance including areas not subject to regulations.

*Signed: CEO, **[Organization's Name]***

Date:

6   PLAN PHASE: COMPLIANCE OBLIGATIONS

Within the planning phase of the EMS it is necessary to consider the issues realised in the previous stages of the EMS, especially the context of the organization; the needs and expectations of stakeholders; and the scope of the EMS. By doing this, the organization will include an assessment of the risks and opportunities that are related to its environmental aspects as well as the Compliance Obligations that need to be addressed. This in turn, should lead to an Action Plan targeted at addressing risks and opportunities facing the organization, as well as intending to achieve the organization's Environmental Objectives.

The organization probably already has some form of EMS with its most mature element most likely being its attention to compliance with relevant laws and regulations. Legal requirements can include national, state and local requirements; permit and license conditions; industry codes of practice and voluntary pledges or commitments made by the organization. Such commitments can include any environmental principles or industry norms that influential stakeholders deem important. Other typical voluntary commitments that give rise to Compliance Obligations can include voluntary codes of practice for safety, risk management and energy efficiency.

An effective EMS can therefore usually build upon what already exists and should include processes to identify and communicate applicable Compliance Obligations and ensure that these requirements are factored into the organization's management efforts. Meeting the organization's Compliance Obligations is one of the main pillars upon which the Environmental Policy should be based because the potential costs of non-compliance, such as possible damage to the environment, revenue loss and the impact on public image and subsequent damage to the organization's brand for example, can be high.

New or revised legal requirements which come into force, as well as external environmental factors such as the effects of climate change, might require modification of subsequent Environmental Objectives or other EMS elements. By anticipating such new regulations and environmental conditions and making changes to the organization's operations to suit, you might avoid coming against future compliance and environmental risks and the costs associated with mitigating such risks. The EMS should therefore include a Procedure for regularly identifying, having access to and analyzing applicable Compliance Obligations. Identifying applicable obligations, interpreting them and determining their impacts upon operations can be a time-consuming task. Fortunately, there are many sources of help easily available for obtaining information about applicable Obligations like laws and regulations, such as:

- Commercial services which often provide emailed bulletins of updated news and online resources.
- National, state and local regulatory agencies.
- Trade groups and associations.
- The Internet.
- Public libraries.
- Seminars and courses.
- Newsletters and magazines.
- Consultants and lawyers.
- Customers, vendors, and other companies.

Answers to the questions provided in Resource 10 can also help you identify applicable Compliance Obligations.

As Compliance Obligations change over time, your organization's Procedure should include a means to ensure that staff are working with up-to-date information and changing the way that they work to suit new, or modified, Obligations.

You can customize the Procedure in Appendix 2: Procedure for Identification of Compliance Obligations to fit your organization's needs.

> *Resource 10 Help in identifying applicable Compliance Obligations*
>
> *Do we have an existing Procedure for identifying applicable Compliance Obligations? If yes, does that Procedure need to be revised? In what way?*
>
> *Who needs to be involved in this Procedure within our organization? What should their responsibilities be?*
>
> *What sources of information do we use to identify applicable Compliance Obligations? Are these sources adequate and effective? How often do we review these sources for possible changes?*
>
> *How do we ensure we have access to Compliance Obligations?*
>
> *How do we communicate information on Compliance Obligations to people within the organization who need this information?*
>
> *Who is responsible for analyzing new or modified legal requirements to determine how we might be affected?*
>
> *How will we keep information on Compliance Obligations updated?*
>
> *Our next step on Compliance Obligations is to...*

Once the applicable environmental requirements have been identified and adopted into the appropriate operations, you will need to contact regulatory agencies with jurisdiction over your organization to secure these approvals. You can customize the Procedure provided in Appendix 3: Procedure for Obtaining Agency Approval to secure Agency approval for processes and activities within your organization.

7   Plan phase: Environmental Aspects and Impacts

An Environmental Aspect is an element of an organisation's activities, products or services that interacts with the environment. Environmental Aspects therefore cause a change to occur to the environment. An Environmental Impact is the effect, either positive or negative, of such an Environmental Aspect and so is any change in the environment, whether adverse or beneficial, wholly or partially resulting from an organisation's activities, products or services. All activities within an organisation such as people washing their hands, purchasing raw materials or manufacturing something have an Environmental Impact. Knowing what the Impacts are is only part of the challenge however. As part of an Environmental Management System you need to know where such Environmental Impacts are coming from and how therefore does the organisation interact with the environment? Hence an EMS must include a procedure to identify and assess not only those Environmental Aspects that staff within the organisation can control but you must also consider the whole life-cycle of the organization's activities, products or services, as well as those aspects and impacts occurring under abnormal and emergency situations over which the organization has some influence. These last points are important as your organisation is not expected to manage issues outside its sphere of influence nor be concerned with issues over which it has no control. For example, while your organisation has control over how much water it buys, it does not have much control over the way in which that water is treated by the water supply company. But in some cases, some level of influence over the water treatment process could be asserted. An organisation needs to focus not just upon the Environmental Aspects of its own activities, products or services, but also consider those Aspects from a life cycle perspective too. Therefore it may be possible for you and your organization's staff to work with suppliers to help persuade them to introduce more environmentally beneficial ways of working.

The term 'Aspects' is neutral as an Environmental Aspect can be either positive, such as making a product out of recycled materials or negative, such as discharging toxic materials into a stream. Aspects may also result from past activities such as historic spills of toxic chemicals and abnormal and unplanned working conditions such as during power outages or earthquakes.

Once all the Environmental Aspects have been identified the next stage in developing a robust Environmental Management System is to determine which Environmental Aspects have, or could have, <u>significant</u> impacts. Aspects that have one or more Significant Impacts should be classified as 'Significant Environmental Aspects'. The Aspects classified as 'Significant' will then greatly influence the development of the organisation's EMS as they will become the focus of effort in trying to reduce (in the case of a detrimental impact) or boost (in the case of a positive impact) their Environmental Impact. To help in the identification of relevant Environmental Aspects and Impacts an Environmental Manager will typically rely upon discussing the processes and systems existing within the organization, as well as the life cycle issues external to the organization, with staff who are experts in that work area.

By understanding the inputs and outputs going into and out from each stage of a process or system a 'Process Map', as shown in Figure 6, can be constructed which will help lay people understand what the Environmental Aspects and Impacts are within different processes. When all the Process Maps are put together, the Environmental Aspects and Impacts relevant to the whole organization and the life cycle of its activities, products and services can be better visualized.

When considering the organization's Environmental Aspects consider not just the organization's normal operating conditions, but also times when there could be abnormal conditions such as during planned shutdowns or start-ups, any reasonably foreseeable unplanned emergency situations and also any sporadic supplier and sub-contractor activities. It is also useful to investigate the environmental phenomenon and their associated Impacts shown in Resource 11 to determine if they are appropriate to your EMS.

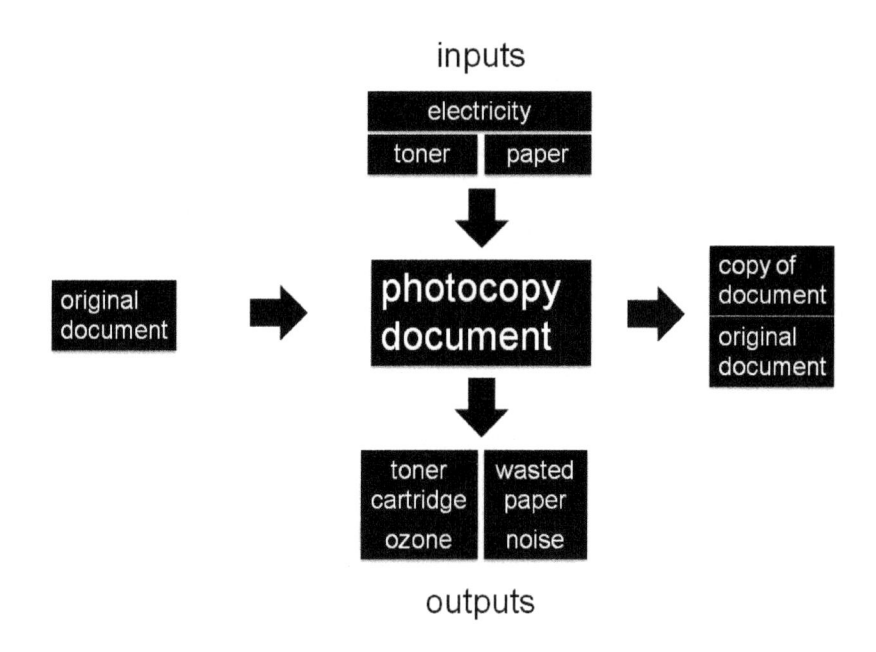

Figure 6 Example process map for photocopying a document

When Environmental Aspects and their related Impacts have been identified you will use this information in setting the organization's Environmental Objectives.

Resource 11 Example Environmental Impacts

Phenomenon	Possible Environmental Impact
Emissions to air	Formation of photochemical smog; human health effects; ozone depletion; global warming and acid rain.
Use of water	Water pollution; damage to aquatic plants and fish; associated damage to land, animal and human health.
Waste management	Wasted resources; compliance with legislation; issues around waste going to landfill.

This does not mean that you need to address all of the Impacts at once as there could be valid reasons why some Impacts can't be wholly addressed, such as the:

- Potential regulatory and legal issues related to the Impact.
- Difficulty and cost of changing systems or processes that are causing the Impact and any effect of such a change on other activities and processes.
- Concerns of influential and powerful stakeholders.
- Effect on the public image of the organisation and its brand.

So as to robustly consider all the issues surrounding each Impact, once the organization's Environmental Impacts have been identified an Environmental Risk Assessment should be undertaken to assess the significance of each Impact. Each negative Environmental Impact poses an element of negative risk to the organization. Assessing significance is achieved by assessing the scale and severity of each Impact, along with its probability of occurrence and likely duration. A scoring system is helpful here whereby the scale, severity, probability and duration of each risk is assessed and combined to give a total score for each Impact. Once all elements for all Impacts have been scored, the total for each Impact is found and consequently all Environmental Impacts can be ranked in order of significance. It may be useful at this stage to split the list of ranked Environmental Impacts into 'action urgently required', 'action required in the short term', and 'no immediate action required' or some other similar grouping which is useful in your organizational context. These categories of Impact can then be color coded into red, amber and green which provides a helpful visual key to lay people enabling a quick, prioritized visualization of the Impacts and their associated risk. An example is shown in Resource 12.

Resource 12 Example Environmental Risk Assessment matrix

Impact	Scale 1 to 5	Severity 1 to 5	Probability 1 to 5	Duration 1 to 5	Significance total scores
Effluent discharge	5	5	5	5	20
Explosion	5	5	1	5	16
Littering	1	1	1	1	4

Key: 1 = low; 5 = high

Such an Environmental Risk Assessment relies upon subjectively quantified data in identifying high risk areas. However it does allow organizations to robustly identify and enable priorities for precious resources which then allow the setting of tangible and useful Environmental Objectives. In this way the allocation of resources aimed at improving environmental performance is achieved in a logical, transparent and defendable way.

PLANNING ACTIONS

Considering the Significant Environmental Aspects, Compliance Obligations, risks and opportunities assessed previously, an EMS requires a clear Plan of Action that addresses each of these identified issues whilst considering the organization's technical options and its financial and other business needs. The Plan should describe how such actions will be integrated and implemented as part of the EMS or other business activities, as well as how the actions will be evaluated with respect to their effectiveness. Such a Plan firstly requires setting Environmental Objectives which once achieved enhances the environmental performance of the organization.

8   PLAN PHASE: ENVIRONMENTAL OBJECTIVES

From the organization's Environmental Policy and the subsequent evaluation of its Environmental Aspects and Environmental Impacts flows a framework for setting and reviewing Environmental Objectives – as shown in Figure 7.

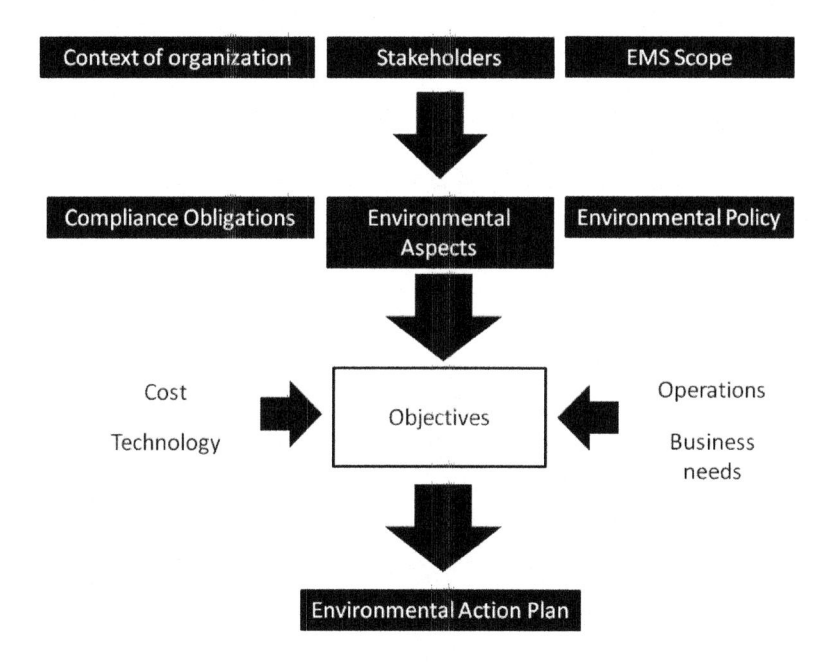

Figure 7 Elements influencing Environmental Objectives setting

An Environmental Objective is a quantifiable overall environmental goal, arising from the Environmental Policy and is something that can be measured, monitored, communicated and updated as appropriate. Some examples of Environmental Objectives and associated ways to achieve them are shown in Resource 13.

> *Resource 13 Example Environmental Objectives and an Action Plan to achieve them*
>
> *Reduce energy use by 10% within the next year by reducing electricity use by 10% by [put date here] and reducing natural gas use by 15% by **[put date here]**.*
>
> *Reducing hazardous chemicals use by 25% within the next year by reducing use of high-VOC paints by 25% by [put date here] and by eliminating use of VOCs by **[put date here]**.*
>
> *Improve employee awareness of environmental issues before the end of the year by holding monthly awareness training courses and by training all staff by **[put date here]**.*

Environmental Objectives are key parts of an EMS as they translate positive environmental intention into action and can be applied across the organization, or to individual business units, or departments depending upon where the implementing actions are needed. Also remember that it is the organization's staff who should determine which Objectives are appropriate and that the appropriateness of such Objectives could change over time and in different contexts.

When developing and setting Environmental Objectives keep in mind the Environmental Policy as this sets the framework and guiding principles for the rest of the Environmental Management System. Also important to address are the organization's Significant Environmental Aspects and all applicable Compliance Obligations placed upon the organization and its operations. Especially important in this last context are the views of stakeholders – people like local authority inspectors and regulators, all of whom ensure that legal and other compliance requirements are met. Chapter 10 has more on this. The views of customers and lobby groups are also important to consider - after all, if customers want changes made to products or services then to remain in business an organization must respond. Balanced with these views is the practicability of change and what is actually achievable within the current business context. An Objective won't be achieved if it's impossible to do right now.

To develop the Environmental Objectives and subsequent Action Plan, it's usually best to involve people in the relevant functional area(s), as these people are the ones tasked with establishing, planning for and achieving these Objectives. Involving people also has the additional benefit of helping to build commitment to the EMS and can even instil a sense of competition as some department managers may want to appear to be better than others in achieving. Senior managers must also be committed to the Environmental Objectives as this ensures adequate resources are available and that Objectives are integrated with other organizational goals.

Objectives can be established to <u>maintain</u> current levels of performance as well as to <u>improve</u> performance. For some Environmental Aspects there may be both maintenance, as well as improvement, Objectives. The Action Plan coming from the Objectives should be sufficiently clear to enable adherence to the plan to be measured and monitored – e.g. a reduction in fossil fuel consumption of 10% next year compared to this year.

There are no 'standard' Environmental Objectives that make sense for all organizations at all times. Rather Environmental Objectives should reflect what the organization does, how well the organization is performing and what it wants to achieve, as is set-out in its Environmental Policy.

Communicate the progress in achieving Objectives across the organization via regular progress reports in formats and media appropriate to your organization. Consider holding an 'open house' or establishing a focus group with people in the community to get the views of interested parties which are outside the organization. This will make your neighbors and other stakeholders feel part of the process and will provide the organization with useful feedback on what issues should be considered as significant. Events like these raise the profile of the organization, aids business transparency and enables people who may not fully understand what the organization does or what challenges it faces to better appreciate the risks, opportunities and threats facing the organization.

9   PLAN PHASE: ENVIRONMENTAL ACTION PLAN

An important part of the planning effort that goes into developing an Environmental Management System is defining what the organisation intends to achieve. To do this the organizational Environmental Objectives are built into an Action Plan, as are the risks and opportunities relevant to the organization and the actions required to address them.

The Plan should describe how the organization will translate its goals and Policy commitments into concrete actions so ensuring that its Environmental Objectives are achieved. To ensure the Environmental Action Plan's effectiveness, within the Plan should be defined the responsibilities, the means and the time frame for achieving the goals, the resources required and how the results will be achieved. Keep in mind that the Plan is a dynamic one and so modifications will be necessary whenever any Environmental Objectives are modified, added or removed; Compliance Obligations are introduced or changed; substantial progress in achieving the Objectives has, or has not, been made or the organization's products, services, processes or facilities change.

To be most effective and efficient Environmental Action Plans need to be coordinated and integrated with other organizational plans, strategies and budgets. For example if there are plans for a major expansion of the organization then it may make sense to look at the possible environmental issues associated with this operational expansion at the same time as developing the Plan.

Build on the plans and programs you currently have for keeping legally compliant as well as those which focus upon health and safety or quality management as this will help to expedite the planning for, and implementation of, an Environmental Action Plan. Involving staff early in establishing the Plan will also help, although it is important here to clearly communicate expectations and responsibilities defined in the Plan to those people who need to know about them. In some cases an Environmental Action Plan may encompass several existing Operating Procedures or Work Instructions. In other cases however, new Operating Procedures or Work Instructions will be required to implement the Plan. Coordinating the Environmental Action Plan with other plans and strategies in this way can exploit some significant cost-saving opportunities. Don't forget to re-evaluate the Plan when considering changes to the organization's activities, products, services, processes, facilities or materials and make this re-evaluation part of your normal change management process.

ENVIRONMENTAL REVIEW FOR NEW PRODUCTS, PROCESSES AND ACTIVITIES

Change is an important part of survival for most organizations. Products, technologies and ways of doing things are regularly updated. To avoid creating a flurry of new Significant Environmental Aspects that must be addressed within the EMS it is helpful to integrate new processes, products and activities into the environmental efforts that are developed for the rest of the organization. This is achieved by setting up a Procedure for reviewing new processes, products or activities while they are in the planning stage. The Procedure should include a checklist to circulate among the people responsible for, or affected by, the new process or product, including those responsible for the area of the organization where the new process or activity will be implemented.

The use of Resource 14 can help in planning for and implementing the Environmental Action Plan whilst a customizable Procedure for establishing Environmental Action Plans is included in Appendix 4: Procedure for Environmental Aspects, Objectives, and Action Plans.

A customizable Procedure for Environmental Reviews is provided in Appendix 5: Procedure for Environmental Review for New Purchases, Processes and Products, along with an example of a checklist – an example extract of one is shown in Appendix 6:

Environmental Management Systems | 57

Environmental Impact Assessment Evaluation Checklist - which can be used for new purchase, process and product reviews.

> *Resource 14 Questions, the answers to which can help in planning for and implementing an Environmental Action Plan*
>
> *Do we have an existing Procedure for establishing Environmental Action Plans? If yes, does that Procedure need to be revised and if so, in what way?*
>
> *What is the basis for our Environmental Action Plans (for example, do they consider our Environmental Objectives, our Environmental Policy commitments and other organizational priorities)?*
>
> *Who needs to be involved in the design and implementation of these Plans within the organization?*
>
> *When is the best time for us to establish and review such Plans? Can this effort be linked to an existing organization Procedures?*
>
> *How do we ensure that changes to products, Procedures, equipment and infrastructure are considered in our Plans?*
>
> *How will we otherwise keep our Plans up-to-date?*
>
> *Our next step on Environmental Action Plans is to...*

10   Do phase: Support

The support required for a successful EMS requires adequate resources, staff competence, awareness, good, effective communication and well-kept documents, as shown in Figure 8.

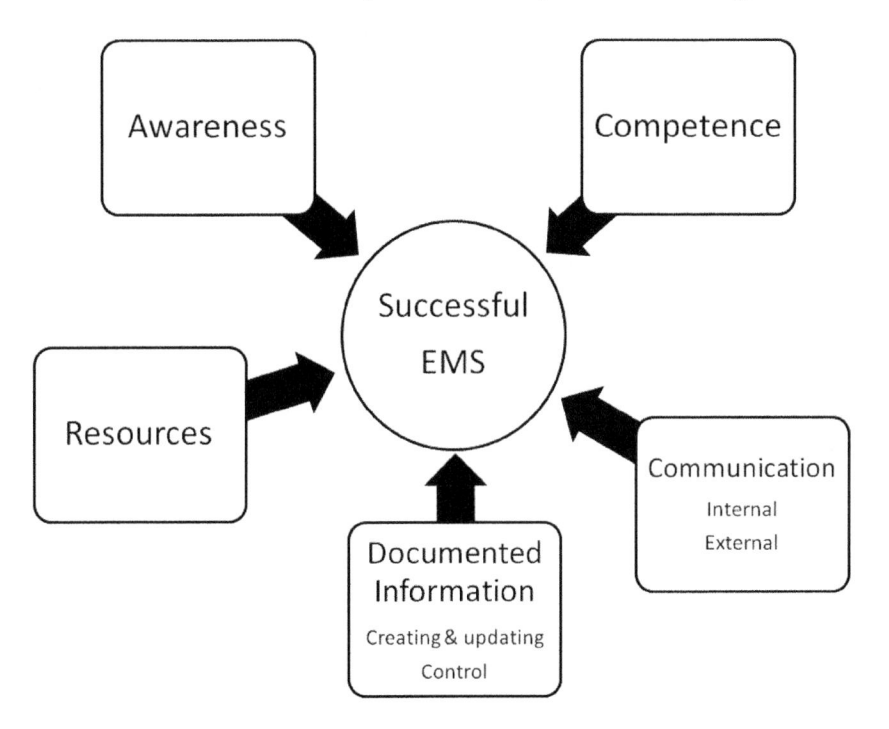

Figure 8 Support for an EMS comes from a mix of adequate resources, staff competence and awareness, effective communication and well managed documents

Resources

For an EMS to be successfully designed, implemented, maintained and continually improved, the organization has to commit resources to such a project. It is therefore necessary for staff to firstly determine what sorts of resources are required; things like staff and materiel. It is then necessary to ensure such resources are provided in appropriate quantities, at the right times and in the right places.

COMPETENCE AND AWARENESS

The activity of every employee has an impact on the environmental performance of the organization and reducing the negative, and enhancing the positive, environmental impacts really means changing people's behaviour. This in turn requires raising peoples' awareness, training people on how to enhance their behaviour and enabling them to acquire new skills ensuring that they are competent in their role(s). After all, employees can only give their best if they understand the decisions that affect them and how their contribution will make a difference. They also then need to be mobilized and given authority to affect positive change.

There are two main reasons to train staff on the organization's Environmental Management System:

- Every person can affect the organization's environmental performance or can help fulfil the organization's Compliance Obligations; and
- Any member of staff can have good ideas about how to improve the organization's environmental performance. Therefore each person within the organization can play an important role in environmental management.

For these reasons the Environmental Training Program should include all staff. Every employee should be aware of the Environmental Policy, the Significant Environmental Aspects that are appropriate to their work activities, key EMS roles and responsibilities of staff within the organization, the environmental Procedures that apply to their work and the importance of conformance with EMS requirements. All personnel should therefore receive appropriate training and support which is tailored to the different needs of staff working at different levels of seniority and different functional groups within the organization.

Training is however just one element of establishing someone's competence at doing their job, as competence comes from a combination of education, training and experience. For tasks that can cause Significant Environmental Aspects, criteria should be established which can be used to measure the competence of individuals performing such critical tasks. Training is therefore needed both in technical work and for raising the environmental-awareness-raising of staff. Task-specific training should also be offered as a subset of general environmental awareness training. As part of an Environmental Management System two types of training are usually therefore required. Baseline training, which is about knowledge and attitudes, and specific training which is bespoke to job functions and dependent upon context:

- Awareness or 'Baseline' training which should be provided to all staff within the organisation and includes the Environmental Policy; and the importance to the organization of the EMS. The environmentally-related roles within the organisation in achieving and maintaining the EMS also need to be described, as well as explaining to staff the consequences of deviations from the EMS with respect to EMS-related Compliance Obligations; and
- Specific technical and skills training for individuals responsible for the specific activities or processes that may create Significant Environmental Aspects and their associated Environmental Impacts.

You can probably already identify some general training needs, but you need to return to this part of the Environmental Management System to add specific technical training needs that may become apparent as you proceed with developing the EMS. For example, Training Plans developed during the evaluation of Operational Controls are likely to be process-specific and should be integrated with the training identified in this part of the EMS.

Developing a Training Plan requires elements of preparation and identifying training needs. This then leads to defining the training objectives; developing training course content; identifying available training materials; implementing the training program; and evaluating the changes in behaviour that have arisen as a result of the training.

To help with identifying training needs consider what the competences staff need are; what are the current levels of education, training and experience of staff and are there gaps between the competence profile and existing staff competences? If there are gaps, these need plugging with appropriate training. Also, if there have been new or changed Procedures or Work Instructions recently introduced within the organization, new and appropriate training will be required.

Using answers to the questions provided in Resource 15 can help identify the organization's Environmental Training Program needs.

Environmental Management Systems | 63

> *Resource 15 Questions, the answers to which can help to begin the process of identifying environmental competence requirements.*
>
> *Do we have an existing process for ensuring environmental competence? If so, does that process need to be revised? In what way(s)?*
>
> *What types of training do we provide now?*
>
> *How would EMS-related training fit with the existing training program?*
>
> *Who is responsible for training now? Who else might need to be involved?*
>
> *How do we determine training needs now? Are these processes effective?*
>
> *Who is responsible for ensuring that employees receive appropriate training?*
>
> *How do we track training to ensure we are on target?*
>
> *How do we evaluate training effectiveness?*
>
> *How do we establish staff competency, where needed?*
>
> *What are the key job functions and activities where we need to ensure environmental competency?*
>
> *Do we have a staff mentoring scheme?*
>
> *Do we need to contract-in competent people?*
>
> *Our next step on training and competence is to...*

Within an EMS, staff working for the organization are required to acquire appropriate levels of competence. As part of the EMS an evaluation of such actions taken to achieve better levels of competency is also required. So don't forget that training is not the only way to ensure environmental competence. Mentoring staff can also boost competence, as can the reassignment of staff or hiring and contracting competent people.

Sometimes training can be undertaken by in-house experts. At other times external trainers may provide better value for money. For example, when designing training in how to competently operate new machinery. When assessing who is to be the trainer, not only does their knowledge and experience matter, but also how skilled and adept they are in communicating concepts appropriately to their learners.

Training will only be effective if appropriate training methods are used. For example lectures are most suited to giving a general overview and introduction to new ideas. 'On the job' training is more practical in nature and is effective for activities combining knowledge, skills and practical techniques. Whatever Training Program is used, an evaluation of the effectiveness of the training is required to assess its usefulness in achieving its objectives and ultimately enhancing the organization's environmental performance. What are required therefore are appropriate performance indicators for the training given. When planning training don't only evaluate short-term effectiveness as new skills and changed behaviours may be abandoned if not practised and supported and then old habits can easily return. A re-evaluation of the training to assess its long-term effectiveness is therefore also required.

You can customize the Procedure provided in Appendix 6: Environmental Impact Assessment Evaluation Checklist and its supporting information shown in Resource 16 and Resource 17 to help you develop your organization's environmental training needs.

Resource 16 Training Needs Analysis — Environmental Courses

What sort of course is required?

Who needs training?

What is the training source?

How long will the training take?

How can the short- and long-term effectiveness of the training be monitored?

How frequent is the training?

Resource 17 Training Needs Analysis — Procedures by area or department

For each change made to existing Procedures, describe the following information:

Identification – for example: Procedure Title

Production process or area affected – for example: Metal working and cutting; Surface preparation; Welding; Painting

Organization support department affected - for example: Purchasing; Plant maintenance; Fuel transfer; Chemical storage; Administration

Training required: **[Outline specific training requirements here]**

COMMUNICATION

This part of the book helps you identify the stakeholders you may want to include in the EMS, the potential benefits of including stakeholders and tips for better communications with stakeholders.

Most employees tend to be interested at some level in the organization in which they work and can therefore provide support for the EMS development. Customers, suppliers and neighbors of the organization can also sometimes provide useful inputs into the EMS. In addition, establishing partnerships with trade associations, suppliers, professional associations, universities and other interested third parties can also be helpful in developing and maintaining the EMS.

An Environmental Management System should define, put in place and keep up-to-date the means for proactive internal and external communications that are relevant to the EMS. The Communications Plan should consider what, when, how and with whom to communicate. See Figure 9.

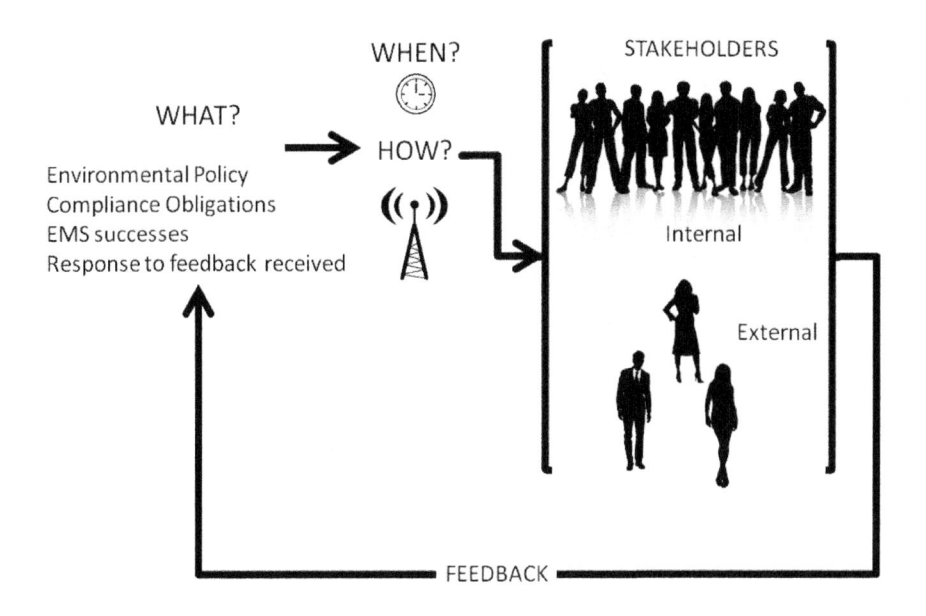

Figure 9 Elements comprising an Environmental Communications Plan

An organization's Communication Plan should therefore identify, explain and communicate environmental Compliance Obligations to all its relevant stakeholders. Such Plans should also provide information about the organization's Environmental Programs and its accomplishments and provide a means for external and internal stakeholders to comment about the EMS and contribute to continuous improvement measures.

IDENTIFYING WHICH STAKEHOLDERS TO COMMUNICATE WITH

Almost every organization will have a wide array of internal and external groups that may be interested in, and helpful partners of, that organization. These groups will not be homogenous as each will have its own priorities and perspectives and each will have something different to contribute to the EMS. Part of the communication-focussed EMS-related work is in identifying and understanding these groups of people and what is important to them with respect to the EMS.

You may want to start by communicating with those stakeholders who have expressed interest in your operations and their associated Environmental Impacts. If you desire additional input into the EMS you can also take the following steps to find other suitable stakeholders:

- Ask your staff, customers, sub-contractors and suppliers.
- Obtain suggestions from local officials.
- Contact the local planning agency.
- Get input from a national advocacy group regarding local or national groups that may be appropriately interested.

STAKEHOLDER ROLES

Before engaging with stakeholders, be clear on what you expect them to do. Consider that internal stakeholder participation can facilitate implementation of environmental projects as employees take ownership of the EMS and the changes it may bring. Different stakeholders also bring useful alternative perspectives to environmental issues, often identifying issues that may otherwise have been overlooked and/or offering satisfying solutions to upcoming challenges.

Participation by all types of stakeholders can add credibility, transparency and value to your EMS whilst involving external stakeholders can help them understand your organization's operating constraints. Forming partnerships with customers and suppliers can also help to identify shared concerns and ways to co-operate to resolve them. Forming partnerships with suppliers can help your organization obtain important information otherwise unobtainable and can help you meet your EMS goals. There may be ways that your organization can also help your customers meet their environmental management needs too. Sometimes just by being an environmental leader creates customer recognition and loyalties, whilst involving customers in the EMS can also help them recognize your leadership and enhance your brand.

HOW TO WORK WITH STAKEHOLDERS

Your stakeholders' concerns may be different from what you expect and may sometimes be less difficult to resolve than you may think. The only way to find out is to communicate with them. Bear in mind that when working with stakeholders effective communication will also facilitate the smooth implementation of your EMS. Resource 18 describes some tips for good communication.

PRIORITIZING STAKEHOLDERS

You may have a long list of people and organizations who are stakeholders within your organization. Some of these may have the power either to block or to advance your environmental work. Some may be interested in what you are doing whilst others may not care. Categorise the stakeholders identifying their power over, and interest in, the environmental performance of the organisation. See Resource 19.

Resource 18 Some tips for effective communications

Begin early in the EMS process. Let people know what you are doing. In most cases you will need the co-operation of several people within your organization to gather information and develop an EMS. Early communication will pay off in greater acceptance of the resulting System.

Set communication objectives. Decide what you want to achieve. Setting goals will help you get the right message across without overwhelming people with too much information and spending too much time. It is helpful to create an EMS Communication Procedure for your organization. The Procedure should outline what kinds of information will be communicated to external stakeholders and how the organization will record and respond to communications from external stakeholders.

Communicate regularly and integrate EMS communications with other efforts. To build support for the EMS, communicate updates regularly. This can usually be accomplished without straining resources — for example, use existing ways to communicate such as bulletin board and intranet postings, email messages or the organization's newsletter.

Ensure that stakeholder dialogue is a two-way process. Stakeholders want to know that their concerns are being heard and taken into account. Convey that your organization is genuinely interested in their input and explain how you include them.

Track communication. Develop a way to record and respond to stakeholder communication. Also appoint a person to be responsible for carrying out the Communication Procedure.

When prioritizing stakeholders, their level of interest is scored out of 3 where 3 = High; 2 = Medium; and 1 = Low. Power refers to the quantity of resources: Human, (H), Financial, (F) and Political, (P) available to stakeholders and their ability to mobilise them. These are scored 5 for 'Very strong' to 1 for 'Very weak'. Total Power is found by adding the 'resources' scores, H+F+P. The overall total is then found by multiplying Interest and Power scores.

Resource 19 Stakeholder Analysis

Stakeholder	Evaluation Criteria					Total = Interest x Power
	Interest	Influence			Total Power	
		H	F	P	H + F + P	
Supply chain	3	5	5	4	14	42
Staff	3	2	3	2	7	21
Auditors	2	2	3	3	8	16

Using the four categories of high and low power, and high and low interest the relative positions of the stakeholders can then be placed in a matrix in which the horizontal axis is labelled interest (from low on the left, to high on the right) and the vertical axis labelled from low power at the bottom to high power at the top – see Figure 10. By doing this the ways to engage with these stakeholders becomes clear as you need to manage closely those with both high power and high interest. These are the people you must fully engage with and make the greatest efforts to satisfy.

For those with high power and low interest you need to communicate sufficiently with these people to keep them satisfied but not so much that they become bored with your message. You should keep those with low power and high interest adequately informed and talk to them to ensure that no major issues are arising as these people can often be helpful with the detail of your environmental work. Whilst those with low power and low interest should be monitored, but not bored with excessive communication.

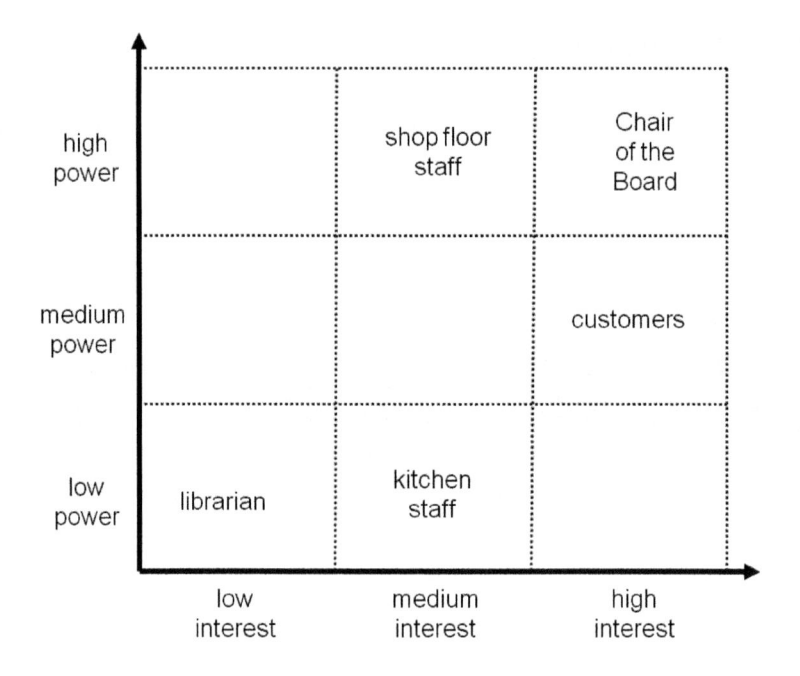

```
high
power                    shop floor        Chair
                         staff             of the
                                           Board

medium                                     customers
power

low         librarian    kitchen
power                    staff

            low          medium            high
            interest     interest          interest
```

Figure 10 Power and Interest Stakeholder Matrix

UNDERSTANDING KEY STAKEHOLDERS

You now need to know more about your key stakeholders, i.e. those interested people who have power over the EMS and are influential in decision-making. You should try to understand how they feel about the EMS project and investigate the best way to engage them in your environmental work. To better understand the needs of your stakeholder consider the questions shown in Resource 20 Questions, the answers to which can help you understand stakeholder needs:

Resource 20 Questions, the answers to which can help you understand stakeholder needs

What financial or other interest do these people have in the outcome of your environmental work? Is it positive or negative? What information do they want from you? How do they want to receive such information?

What is their current opinion of your work? Is it based on good information?

Who influences their opinions? Do some of these influencers therefore become important stakeholders?

If some stakeholders are unlikely to think positively about the EMS, what will win them around to support your EMS project? If you don't think you will be able to win them around how will you manage their opposition?

Who else might be influenced by their opinions? Do these people become stakeholders in their own right?

A good way of answering these questions is to talk to stakeholders as they are likely to be open about their views and asking people's opinions is often the first step in building a successful relationship with them. It is helpful to then summarize your understanding so that you can see the blockers or critics, advocates and supporters of your EMS. A way of doing this is by colour coding the stakeholders on the Stakeholder Power and Interest Matrix (an example is shown in Figure 10 Power and Interest Stakeholder Matrix): show advocates and supporters in green, blockers and critics in red and others who are neutral in orange. You can then use Resource 21 to help you plan how to communicate about the EMS with your organization's stakeholders.

> *Resource 21 Questions, the answers to which help develop stakeholder communications*
>
> *Who are our external stakeholders? How were these stakeholders identified? With regard to our organization what are the key concerns of these stakeholders? How do we know this?*
>
> *What community outreach efforts are we making now and have made in the past? How successful were these efforts?*
>
> *What methods do we use for external communications? Which are the most effective?*
>
> *How do we gather and analyze information to be communicated? Who has responsibility for this?*
>
> *How do we communicate internally, as well as with our suppliers and contractors? What Procedures do we have to respond to internal inquiries? How effective are these methods?*
>
> *Our next step on communication is to...*

Resource 22 can then be used to plan stakeholder EMS-related communications. You can customize Appendix 8: Procedure for Communicating With Stakeholders whilst the supporting form, Resource 23 Record of External Stakeholder Communication, can be used to track communications.

If the organization receives communications from a stakeholder about the EMS, then it is a requirement of the EMS that an appropriate response is made. How this is done depends upon the type of communication received, as well as the specific topic of the communication.

Resource 22 Communications Program Matrix

Stakeholder(s):

Potential environmental interest:

What we want to tell them:

What we want them to tell us:

How we will tell them:

When we will do it:

Person responsible:

Resource 23 Record of External Stakeholder Communication

Date and time of communication:

Who completed this record?

What type of contact was made?

Which environmental issue or concern was discussed?

Which actions need to be taken?

What type of follow-up is required?

Documented Information

The Documented Information within an EMS usually takes the form of an EMS Manual that is available throughout the organization and which outlines the whole EMS plus all of its supporting information. Maintaining an EMS Manual is important as it provides:

- Consistency. Information spread by word-of-mouth is rarely communicated consistently, whereas written information is more likely to be consistent when passed between people, as well as maintaining such consistency over time. In most organizations change is a fact of life — new projects are undertaken, the organization grows and employees change positions or leave the organization. Accurate documentation will make it much easier to maintain an effective and flexible EMS during these changes.
- Assessment of progress towards environmental improvements. Creating EMS documentation helps staff assess the progress of the EMS. Some inconsistencies in the System may also appear only as you commit ideas to paper and having such a record will allow you to check on progress and evaluate results.
- Demonstration of environmental performance. If you want to certify your EMS or enter a recognition program, staff must demonstrate that the EMS is complete and functioning correctly. EMS documentation is used as part of the evidence that demonstrates this.

An EMS Manual provides an overview and description of the pieces and links between all parts of the EMS. At a minimum the EMS Manual should describe core elements of the Environmental Management System and show how the elements interact, providing links to related Documented Information. This usually includes the following EMS elements:

- Environmental Policy.
- Organizational chart which describes key staff responsibilities.
- A description of how the organization satisfies EMS requirements.
- System-level Procedures.
- Activity- or process-specific Operational Control Procedures and Work Instructions.
- Other EMS-related Documented Information such as Emergency Preparedness and Response Plans.

In its entirety EMS Documented Information describes the make-up of the system i.e., what the organization does with respect to its environmental performance and how staff carry out EMS-related duties, as well as demonstrating the environmentally-beneficial actions the EMS information describes are being undertaken.

The EMS Manual does not need to describe every detail of the EMS, and so try to keep EMS documentation simple. Instead the Manual can provide references to other documents and Procedures. EMS documentation should be updated as needed, when modifications are made to the System.

Appendix 9: EMS Manual can then be used as a template for your EMS Manual.

The first thing to do at this stage of EMS development is to determine how the EMS documents you need can be integrated with Documented Information that already exists in the organization. Find out what environmentally-related documentation already exists, what its purpose is and whether it works. Using the same format for all Documented Information will make it easier for people to use the documents. Use Resource 24 as a guide in developing your organization's EMS documentation.

> *Resource 24 Questions, answers to which help develop EMS documentation*
>
> *Do we have existing documentation for our EMS? If yes, how is this EMS documentation maintained?*
>
> *Who is responsible for maintaining the EMS documentation?*
>
> *What does our EMS documentation consist of?*
>
> *Do we have an EMS Manual that describes the EMS? If so does it describe the links among System elements?*
>
> *Is our EMS documentation integrated with other organizational documentation? If so how do we ensure proper coordination between environmental and other functions?*
>
> *How will we keep our EMS documentation up-to-date?*
>
> *How will we keep our EMS documentation secure?*
>
> *Our next step on EMS documentation is to...*

The second step in this stage of EMS development is to customize the documentation to meet the organization's needs. You will probably need to make a compromise between the documentation production needs and the available budget.

You also need to consider if the organization operates in a single, or multiple, location(s) as this will affect who creates some of the Documented Information and where it is located. It may also affect how many versions of a document are necessary to cover different circumstances. Many organizations use an electronic system to maintain Documented Information especially as cloud computing has become so ubiquitous, relatively safe and cheaply available. Care must be taken though as whilst computer systems are handy they can often easily be accessed by a number of people and so there are risks that electronic documentation can be edited or destroyed – sometimes maliciously, sometimes accidentally. Adequate levels of security, or at least restrictions on who can change data, is therefore a critical issue for organizations that use electronic documentation systems.

Before developing any EMS documents, plan the best format and media for them. If an organization standard exists, use it. If such a standard doesn't exist, the need for EMS documentation provides an opportunity to create a standard organizational format and choose the appropriate media. When designing the system consider whether text is single or double line spaced and why; choose margins, header, footer, typefaces, text and headings and include plans for bulleted and numbered lists, tables and paragraph spacing. This is appropriate for both paper- and electronically-based formats. Once you have a consistent format for documents, ensure people use it. All EMS documents will then look like part of an organized and integrated System and will be easier to read and understand. Not all documentation needs to, or should, be text – choose an appropriate media for the target audience. Some organizations use signs above the appropriate equipment for some Work Instructions (like a 'no littering' sign around a campus). Sometimes bilingual text may be needed. Whatever your organizational context is consider the needs of the EMS users — if the message is not understood, it will never be implemented.

Once all the above steps are complete you can then prototype each document. Prototyping helps you visualize what you will need in the document as well as helping you to create an outline for it before you actually have sufficient information to complete the document. This is like drafting a document, but only in outline. As you consider what is needed for the document in this way you also gain an understanding about what you may need to support the EMS. The best people to prototype documents are the people who will use them. Involving them in the process helps ensure that the

Documented Information is usable and also valuable in supporting the EMS.

To help plan your organization's EMS Documented Information consider the questions in Resource 25 for each of the EMS-related Documented Information you have identified as being required, as well as the process in Figure 11.

Resource 25 Questions, answers to which will help you develop information you'll need to document as part of your EMS.

What is the document's purpose?

Who will use the document and how?

What format(s) should it be in?

What must be included in the document?

How long should the document be?

Which information is most critical?

How can information be best arranged?

Is the information process-focused? Focussing upon a process helps people who use the information to better understand how their jobs fit into the organization's other functions.

The purpose of documenting information and managing it is to demonstrate that the organization is actually implementing the EMS as it was intended. While Documented Information provides value to staff you also may need to provide the information to external stakeholders as evidence of proper EMS implementation.

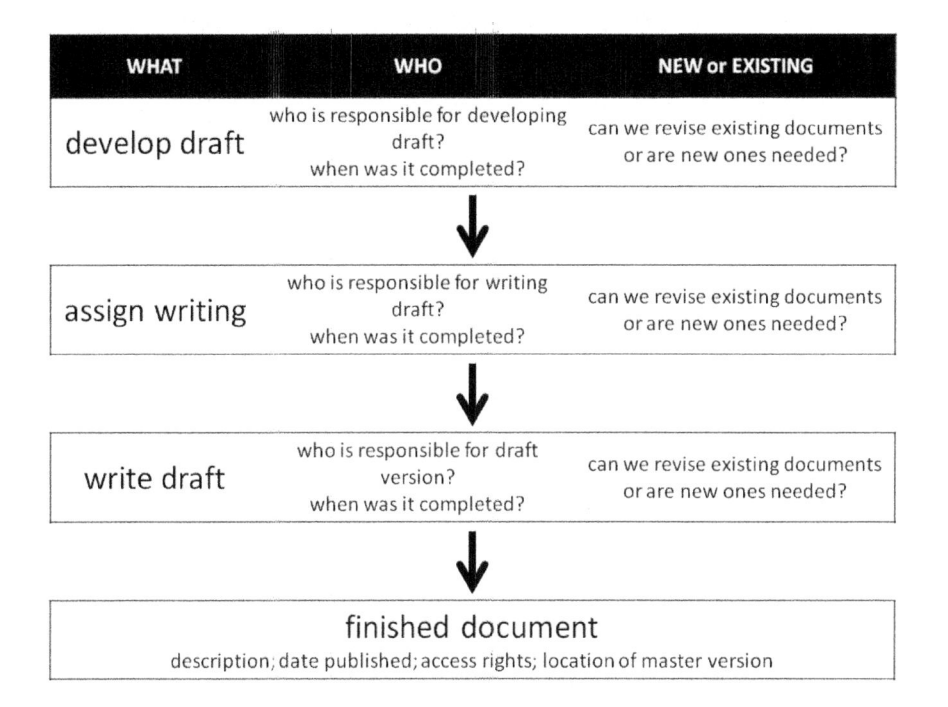

WHAT	WHO	NEW or EXISTING
develop draft	who is responsible for developing draft? when was it completed?	can we revise existing documents or are new ones needed?
assign writing	who is responsible for writing draft? when was it completed?	can we revise existing documents or are new ones needed?
write draft	who is responsible for draft version? when was it completed?	can we revise existing documents or are new ones needed?
finished document description; date published; access rights; location of master version		

Figure 11 How to develop EMS documentation

Documented Information management is sometimes seen as bureaucratic, but it is difficult to imagine a robust EMS operating consistently without accurate Documented Information. This is because Documented Information provides evidence that the Procedures that make up the EMS are being implemented correctly. The tasks involved in this part of the EMS are to decide which documents you will keep, how you will keep them and for how long they should be kept. You should also decide how to dispose of Documented Information once they are no longer needed. If your organization has a Quality Management System you should already have a procedure in place for managing Documented Information. This procedure could be adapted for EMS purposes.

Examples of the types of Documented Information you might keep are:

- Details of Compliance Obligations.
- Organization chart.
- The organization's Environmental Policy.
- EMS audit and Compliance Obligation audit reports.
- Hazardous material spill and other incident reports.
- Job descriptions and performance evaluations.
- Permits, licenses and other approvals.
- Reports of identified nonconformities, Corrective Action Plans and corrective action tracking data.
- Reports of progress towards meeting Environmental Objectives.
- Results of Environmental Aspects identification.
- Samples of organization-specific Environmental Policies and Procedures.
- Samples of supporting documentation for reporting and communication networks, such as meeting notices, meeting minutes and memoranda.
- Samples of written Environmental Management Program performance and status reports.
- Training records related to EMS competence.

Resource 26 provides a checklist of things to think about when establishing a Documented Information Management Procedure.

Appendix 10: Procedure for Environmental Documented Information is customizable and can be used to manage your organization's EMS documented Information. The following list shows the Documented Information which need to be tracked with respect to when they are created, replaced and made obsolete:

- Identification of Compliance Obligations.
- EMS Responsibilities.

- Identification and Significance Determination of Environmental Aspects and Setting Objectives.
- Stakeholder Communication Record.
- Environmental Management Action Plan.
- Index of Environmental Documented Information.
- Training Needs Analysis—Environmental Courses.
- Training Needs Analysis—Procedures and Work Instructions by Area/Department.
- Project Environmental Checklist.
- Master Document List.
- Corrective Action Request.
- Corrective Action Tracking Log.
- Environmental Briefing Packet and Contractor Method Statement Template.
- Internal EMS Audit Checklist.
- Internal EMS Audit Schedule Form.
- Management Review Record.

> *Resource 26 Issues to consider when establishing a Documented Information Management Procedure*
>
> *Identify which EMS Documented Information are required as part of your organization's EMS Compliance Obligations.*
>
> *Focus upon documents that add value and avoid bureaucracy. If documents have no value or are not specifically required, don't collect them. The information you choose to keep should also be accurate and complete.*
>
> *Establish a Documented Information Retention Policy and ensure that it is upheld. Make sure that the Policy takes into account Documented Information retention requirements specified in applicable Compliance Obligations.*
>
> *Consider who needs access to information and in what circumstances such access is needed.*
>
> *Consider using a suitable format and media for the EMS Documented Information Management System which provides for the rapid retrieval of documents as well as providing appropriate control to such access.*
>
> *Think about which documents might require additional security. Do you need to restrict access to certain Documented Information? Back-up critical information at another location and keep a hard copy of the documents in case of computer system malfunction.*

UPDATING AND CONTROLLING DOCUMENTED INFORMATION

To ensure that personnel are consistently performing their work correctly the organization must provide them with the proper tools. In the context of an EMS this means up-to-date Procedures, Work Instructions and other EMS-related documents. People in your organization probably use various documents such as Procedures,

Work Instructions, forms and drawings as they perform their duties. Staff therefore probably already have some means to manage these documents. You also need to manage documents as part of the EMS, as without a way to manage such EMS documents you can't be sure that people are working with the right tools. So to ensure that everyone is working with the proper EMS documents your organization should have a Procedure that describes how such information is 'controlled'. This means that everyone is using the most updated version of the document. Implementation of this Procedure should ensure that EMS documents can be located; are periodically reviewed to make sure they are still current, are available where needed and removed when they become obsolete. The Document Control Procedure should also address who is responsible for, and is authorized to, prepare documents, make changes to them, keep them updated and ensure they are adequately protected from improper use or loss of integrity.

Don't make the Document Control Procedure more complicated than it needs to be. This can be achieved by limiting distribution, determining how many of each documents are needed and where they should be maintained for easy access by staff. Consider using a paperless system if the people that need access to documents are connected in some way, for example via an intranet system or a cloud-based network. Such systems can considerably facilitate both the control and revision of information.

Prepare a Document Control Index that shows all the EMS documents and the history of their revision. Include this Index in the EMS Manual. If multiple paper copies of documents are available prepare a distribution list showing who has each copy and where the copies are located. Highlight these changes as sometimes changes to documents will be necessary as Procedures or other documents are revised. This will make it easier for readers to find the changes and so ensure that everyone is kept updated. Using Resource 27 Questions, answers to which will help determine your organization's Documentation Control Procedure can be useful at this stage.

Appendix 11: Procedure for Document Control provides a customizable example of a Procedure that describes how EMS documents can be controlled. You can also use Resource 28 as it describes the Policies, Manuals, Plans, Procedures and forms that make the EMS.

Resource 27 Questions, answers to which will help determine your organization's Documentation Control Procedure

Do we have an existing Procedure for controlling EMS documents? If yes, does it need revising?

Who needs access to controlled copies of EMS Documented Information?

How do we ensure that EMS documents are periodically reviewed and updated as necessary?

How do we ensure the EMS documents are adequately protected from loss of confidentiality? From improper use? From loss of integrity?

Who has authority to generate new EMS documents or modify existing ones?

How are users alerted to the existence of new EMS documents or revisions to existing ones?

How do we ensure that obsolete documents are not used?

Is our EMS Document Control Procedure integrated with other functions?

Our next step on document control is to...

Resource 28 Example Master Document List for an EMS Manual

Environmental Policy
EMS Manual
Integrated Spill Plan
Procedure to Identify Compliance Obligations
Compliance Obligations
Procedure for Obtaining Agency Approval
Procedure for Environmental Aspects, Objectives and Action Plan
Identification and Significance Determination of Environmental Aspects and Setting Objectives
Environmental Management Program
Procedure for Communication with Stakeholders
External Stakeholder Communication Record
Procedure for Environmental Documented Information
Index of Environmental Documented Information
Procedure for EMS Management Review
Management Review Record
Procedure for Emergency Preparedness and Response
Procedure for Environmental Competence and Awareness
Training Needs Analysis - Environmental Course
Training Needs Analysis - Procedures by Area/Department
Procedure for Monitoring and Measurement
Procedure for Environmental Review for New Purchases, Processes and Products
Project Environmental Checklist
Procedure for Document Control
Master Document List
Procedure for Corrective Action
Corrective Action Request
Corrective Action Tracking Log
Procedure for Contractors and Sub-contractors
Environmental Brief and Contractor Method Template
Procedure for EMS and Regulatory Compliance Audits
Internal EMS Audit Checklist
Internal EMS Audit Schedule Form

11 Do phase: Operation

OPERATIONAL PLANNING AND CONTROL

To work within your organization's Environmental Policy and Environmental Objectives the operations and activities that are associated with your organization's identified Significant Environmental Aspects must be kept under control. This means that the organization must therefore plan the execution of these activities, along with the maintenance of each activity, to ensure that they are carried out under specified (i.e. 'controlled') conditions by establishing and maintaining appropriate documented Procedures. This is to avoid situations where the absence of such Procedures could lead to deviations from Compliance Obligations, the Environmental Policy or from the organization's Environmental Objectives. All planned changes; procurement activities as well as outsourced processes should be controlled, or where such control is not possible, at least positively influenced. How this is to be achieved should be described in the EMS. The results of unintended changes should also be evaluated leading to the mitigation of any unintended adverse Environmental Impacts.

The organization should establish controls to ensure that its environmental requirements are met in design and development processes, throughout the life cycle of the product/service, not forgetting to consider its environmental requirements from a more holistic life cycle perspective with respect also to procurement, external providers, transport and end-of-life issues – see Figure 12.

These Operational Controls usually take the form of documented Procedures, Work Instructions or best management practices.

For the Significant Environmental Aspects for which you have established Objectives for improvement, the corresponding Environmental Management Action Plan will serve as a form of

Operational Control resulting in improved environmental performance. What are left are Significant Environmental Aspects which the organization must maintain in order to keep within its Compliance Obligations and organizational policy.

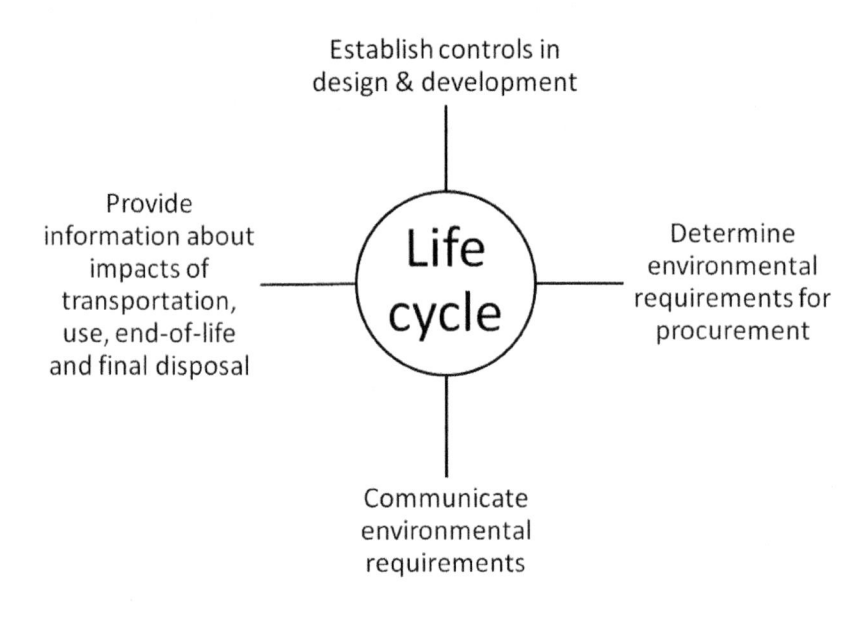

Figure 12 Environmental controls from a life cycle perspective

Most organizations may already have the majority of the necessary compliance-related Operational Controls documented and in place. Even so the job of canvassing the entire organization and its operations to ensure a match between existing Procedures, Work Instructions, best management practices and the list of Significant Environmental Aspects is a crucial one. Likewise, there are two additional tasks required within the Operational Controls stage of an EMS. These are ensuring that the Procedures you have are suitable and filling the gaps that you have identified where new Procedures are required.

Resource 29 gives an example of activity areas and some relevant Operational Controls.

Resource 29 Example List of an Organization's Common Areas of Activity and some Associated Operational Controls

Chemicals storage: *Hazardous Waste Area Inspection, Bulk Storage and Containment, Containerized Material Storage, Hazardous Waste Accumulation, Container Labelling, Hazardous Waste Operations Procedure, Control of Discharges and Waste Manifest.*

Wastewater Management: *Wastewater Handling, Sanitary Waste Disposal and Oily Water Transfer*

Workshops and Maintenance: *Environmental Compliance Assessment and Disposition of Fluorescent Bulbs, Batteries, and Mercury Items.*

Air Quality Management: *Shrouding, Abrasive Blast Containment, Clean-up, and Storage and Tracking of Internal Combustion Emissions Engines.*

DRAFTING OPERATIONAL CONTROLS

Use the questions in Resource 30 to help plan Procedures to cover operational activities and situations where their absence could lead to deviations from Compliance Obligations and/or the Environmental Policy.

> *Resource 30 Questions, answers to which will help in planning EMS Procedures*
>
> *Have we identified all operations associated with Significant Environmental Aspects, and Compliance Obligations? If not, how will this be accomplished? Who should be involved?*
>
> *What operations and activities are associated with our Environmental Objectives? How are the operations and activities controlled? How do we know whether these controls are adequate?*
>
> *How do we train employees and contractors on relevant Operating Controls?*
>
> *If new Controls are needed, or existing ones need to be revised, what is our Procedure for doing so?*
>
> *Who needs to be involved in this Procedure?*
>
> *Our next step on Operational Control is to...*

The customizable Procedure provided in Appendix 12: Procedure for Contractors and Sub-contractors, along with the sample Contractor Environmental Briefing Statement (Resource 49 and Resource 50 in Appendix 12: Procedure for Contractors and Sub-contractors) describes a Procedure for controlling the Environmental Aspects caused by contractors and their sub-contractors who are on-site.

Resource 31 will help you identify needed Procedures for each activity that has an associated Significant Environmental Aspect linked to it and that should be controlled.

> *Resource 31 Worksheet for Determining Which Operations or Activities Require Operational Controls*
>
> *Describe the operation or activity that has Significant Environmental Aspects that needs to be controlled.*
>
> *Is a Procedure needed for this operation/activity?*
>
> *If a Procedure is needed, must it be developed or does a Procedure exist?*
>
> *If one exists, is it already recorded?*
>
> *Who is the contact person for this Procedure?*
>
> *When was this action completed and by whom?*

It is useful to involve people who will work with the Control Procedures in the development of such controls as they are usually knowledgeable in that area of work, sometimes know which systems would be most successful and can help identify efficient and effective practices. You can accomplish this by meeting with staff and have them describe the current Procedures. Discuss the Environmental Objective that is the focus of this part of the EMS and obtain staff input on the appropriate Operational Controls to ensure that the Objective can be met. Also check if there are any current and undocumented Procedures that may partly or entirely fulfil the Environmental Objective. Current Controls may however need to be modified. Have staff and an appropriate manager review the draft Controls and incorporate their input into any required further modifications. Always try to keep written Operational Controls simple and concise. Focus on activities that may lead to Significant Environmental Impacts and avoid getting overwhelmed by trying to control every activity and process.

DESIGNATE RESPONSIBILITY FOR MAINTAINING AND REVIEWING OPERATIONAL CONTROLS

Designate those people responsible for maintaining the Controls and for reviewing them to ensure that Procedures are followed and any deviations from the Procedures are corrected as soon as possible. Generally the staff responsible for a Significant Environmental Aspect will also be responsible for implementing the associated Operational Controls. The immediate line manager would most likely then be responsible for the regular review of the Controls. It is helpful to list those people responsible for each set of Procedures. Resource 32 can help with this.

Resource 32 Worksheet to help link Operational Control Procedures to performance indicators.

What is the Significant Environmental Aspect(s) of concern?

What are the proper performance indicators for the Significant Environmental Aspect?

Which associated job functions are affected by this Significant Environmental Aspect and performance indicator(s)?

Are there existing Operational Control Procedures for this Significant Environmental Aspect or is further Operational Control Procedure development and/or modification needed?

What is the deadline for this work?

Who is the person responsible for this?

Where is the Procedure kept?

Develop Operational Control-related Competence

Achieving success in meeting Environmental Objectives for each Significant Environmental Aspect depends, in part, upon making sure that each person responsible for maintaining or reviewing controls has received adequate training and has the appropriate level of competence. After the Operational Controls are drafted, develop a Training Program that ensures that everyone understands the Controls and their role in ensuring that they are followed.

Resource 33 can be used to help your organization determine its training needs associated with the Operational Controls. It helps identify, plan for and track the training needs of staff and should be combined with general environmental training when creating EMS competency training.

Resource 33 Worksheet for planning environmental training focussed upon an organization's Operational Controls

What is the Significant Environmental Aspect(s) of concern?

What are the existing Operational Control Procedures for this Significant Environmental Aspect(s)?

Who is responsible for the Procedure's implementation?

Does this person/people need training

What is the best way to train these staff?

When is training best to take place, and for how long will it take?

What will the training cost? When will the training be completed?

Who is responsible for the training?

TAKE CORRECTIVE ACTION WHEN OBJECTIVES ARE NOT MET

Taking action to correct failures in Operational Controls as quickly as possible is key in ensuring that the organization meets its Environmental Objectives. Resource 34 Corrective Action Request provides a customizable way to record such corrective actions and Resource 35 provides an example way to help track the progress of such Actions.

Resource 34 Corrective Action Request

In this Action Request, include the following information:

Audited Area/Department

Audit date

Auditor(s)

Description of Non-Conformance

Root Cause Analysis

Corrective Action

Date of Implementation

Verification

EMERGENCY PREPAREDNESS AND RESPONSE

Disasters or emergencies can happen suddenly and when they occur they create situations where normal operations can quickly become overwhelmed, often leading to environmental damage. During such crises organizations require Emergency Procedures that describe how emergency response operations and recovery management will work in such situations, mitigating the negative impacts of the emergency situation.

Resource 35 Corrective Action Tracking Log

For this Log to be effective, include the following information:

Corrective Action Record number

Issue date

Person responsible for Corrective Action

Area

Description

Corrective Action completion date

Overall completion date

Emergency Management is the discipline of avoiding and dealing with risks, as well as preparing, supporting and rebuilding operations after emergencies have occurred. As part of Emergency Management, Environmental Emergency and Accident Preparedness and Response Plans enable the effective management of emergency prevention plans, as well as immediate actions and operations required to respond to an emergency.

Consistent with focussing upon continual improvement it is important to review the organization's emergency response performance after an incident has occurred so that you can correct deficiencies in the Procedure or make other improvements. You can then use the results of such a review to determine if more training is needed or if Emergency Plans and Procedures should be revised.

Some organizations address these requirements through Integrated Contingency Plans that combine the requirements of numerous regulatory programs into one plan.

Emergency Preparedness and Response, (EP&R) Programs should enable staff to:

- Assess the potential for accidents and emergencies.
- Prevent incidents and their associated environmental impacts.
- Respond to incidents if and when they occur.
- Periodically test Emergency Plans and Procedures.
- Review, and revise if necessary, procedures after tests.
- Develop Systems to mitigate the impacts associated with accidents and emergencies.

Getting started

Two planning components that many organizations overlook are how they identify the potential for accidents and emergencies and how they prevent these occurrences or mitigate their impact. The Environmental Management Cross Functional Team can identify most potential emergencies by imagining different emergency scenarios that could occur and which are related to the hazardous materials, activities and processes used within the organization. In addition to normal operations the CFT should also consider the start-up and shutdown stages of equipment and all other abnormal operating conditions to cover any issues peculiar to these phases of operations.

When developing Procedures you need to ensure that everyone, including new employees, knows what to do in an emergency. Communicate with local officials, such as the local fire department and hospital, about potential emergencies at your organization and how they would support your response efforts. Resource 36 can be used to help develop and maintain the EP&R Plans.

Environmental Management Systems | 99

Resource 36 Questions, the answers to which help in the development and maintenance of Emergency Preparedness and Response Plans and Procedures

Have we reviewed our operations and activities for potential emergency situations? If not, how will this be accomplished? Who should be involved?

Do our existing Emergency Plans describe how we will prevent incidents and their associated Environmental Impacts? If not, how will this be accomplished? Who should be involved?

Have we trained personnel on their roles and responsibilities during emergencies?

What emergency equipment do we maintain?

How do we know that emergency equipment is adequate for our needs?

How do contractors and other visitors know what to do in an emergency situation?

When was our last emergency drill?

Is there a plan and schedule for conducting future emergency drills?

Have we established a feedback system to learn from experiences?

Our next step on Emergency Preparedness and Response is...

To help develop your organization's Emergency Preparation and Response Plans conduct training drills to reinforce training and get feedback on the effectiveness of your Procedures. Revise and improve such Procedures as you learn from mock drills, feedback from training or actual emergencies. You could also post copies of your EP&R Procedures around the organization and especially in areas where high hazards exist. Include phone numbers for your on-site Emergency Coordinator, local fire department, local police, hospital and other appropriate people. Finally ensure that your EP&R Procedure describes:

- All appropriate potential emergency situations such as fires, explosions, spills or releases of hazardous materials and natural disasters.
- Hazardous materials used on-site and their locations.
- Key organizational responsibilities such as the Emergency Coordinator.
- Arrangements with local emergency support providers.
- Emergency Response Procedures including Emergency Communications.
- Locations and types of emergency response equipment.
- Maintenance schedule for the emergency response equipment.
- Training and testing of personnel, including the on-site Emergency Response Team if applicable.
- Testing of alarms and public address systems.
- Evacuation routes, exits and assembly points.

A sample EP&R Procedure that you can customize and use for developing your EP&R is included as Appendix 13: Procedure for Emergency Preparedness and Response.

The example Emergency Preparedness and Response Requirements checklist shown in Resource 37 provides a way to list potential emergency scenarios along with their potential impact, required actions and any required Procedures and training.

Resource 37 Emergency Preparedness and Response Requirements checklist

Potential emergency scenario

Potential Environmental Impact(s)

Stakeholders involved

Staff involved

Action required

Procedures needed

Training needed

Training Plan and Schedule

12 CHECK PHASE: PERFORMANCE EVALUATION

The evaluation of the performance of an EMS has three strands: monitoring and measuring; auditing and review, as shown in Figure 13.

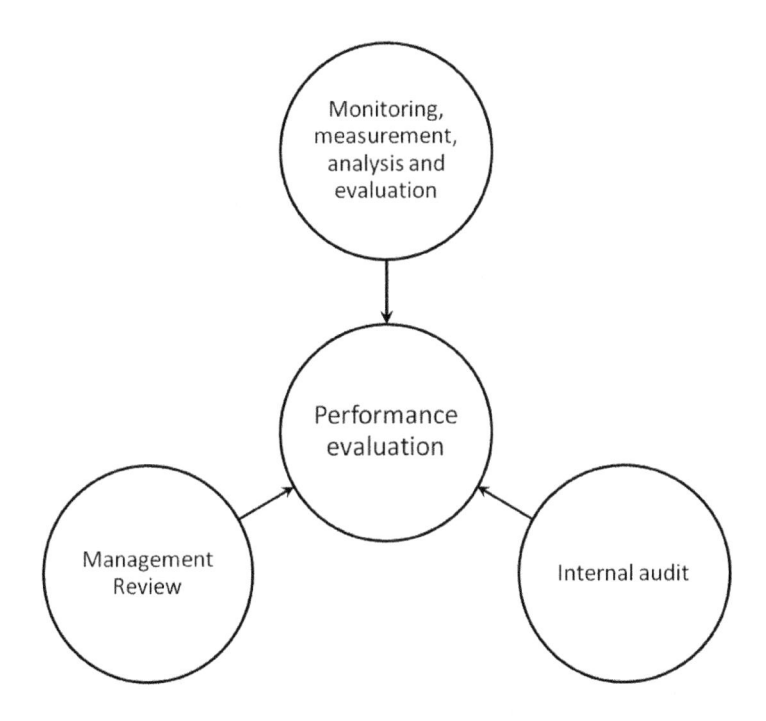

Figure 13 EMS performance evaluation

MONITORING, MEASUREMENT, ANALYSIS AND EVALUATION

An EMS without any effective monitoring, measurement, analysis and evaluation processes is like driving at night without the car headlights on — you know that you are moving but you can't tell where you are going or even if you're heading in the correct direction. Within an EMS, monitoring activities and measuring the inputs and outputs from those activities helps you evaluate the environmental performance of the organization whilst also enabling you to analyze the causes of problems and assess compliance with appropriate obligations that may describe certain performance criteria. In short, monitoring, measurement, analysis and evaluation actions help you manage the organization better. For example the results of pollution prevention and other environmentally-related efforts are easier to demonstrate when current and reliable data are available. Such data also helps demonstrate the value of the EMS to senior managers and so your organization should therefore develop means to monitor the key characteristics of operations and activities that have Significant Environmental Impacts or are required to ensure the organization is acting within legally defined restraints. This will also require the organization to periodically evaluate organizational compliance with its obligations through internal audits. The performance of the EMS, including progress in achieving its Environmental Objectives, will also need to be tracked.

MONITORING EFFICIENTLY

Monitoring, measurement, analysis and evaluation Procedures within the organization can be resource-intensive and so to help you minimize the resources required clearly define the monitoring, measurement, analysis and evaluation needs of the EMS. While collecting meaningful information is clearly important, resist the urge to collect lots of unnecessary data as this will only increase costs unnecessarily. Also review the kinds of monitoring you currently do for regulatory compliance and other purposes, such as Quality or Health and Safety Management as this might also be able to serve EMS purposes. If not, what additional monitoring or measuring might be needed? Start with a relatively simple monitoring, measurement, analysis and evaluation Procedure and then build on it as you gain experience with the EMS. It's better to measure fewer items consistently well than to measure many items inconsistently.

To help establish your organization's monitoring, measurement, analysis and evaluation activities put a Procedure in place to systematically identify, correct and prevent actions that violate EMS Compliance Obligations. Effectiveness of this compliance assessment process should be considered during the EMS Management Review and to help the Review become invaluable, a systematic discovery of violations is to be encouraged. The Review should include the use of performance indicators to monitor and evaluate progress towards achievement, or moves towards non-conformance. This means detecting potential violations through environmental audits or compliance management systems that show that they are reliable in preventing, detecting and correcting such violations. Also consider what information you will need to determine whether the organization is implementing its Operational Controls properly.

Measure progress on achieving Objectives on a regular basis and communicate the results of such measurement to senior managers. To do this select appropriate measurements of the key characteristics that apply to each Environmental Objective ensuring that you can commit the necessary resources to track performance information over time. It is a good idea to start with a small number of these performance indicators and build upon them later as you gain experience. Use your answers to the questions provided in Resource 38 to determine your organization's monitoring, measurement, analysis and evaluation Procedure. Resource 39 is a worksheet to help create an effective Monitoring, Measurement, Analysis and Evaluation Procedure within your organization's EMS. You can also customize Appendix 14: Procedure for Monitoring, Measurement, Analysis and Evaluation to help you monitor and measure Significant Environmental Aspects associated with your organization's operations and activities, to calibrate and maintain monitoring equipment and to evaluate compliance.

Resource 38 Questions, the answers to which will help you determine your organization's EMS monitoring, measurement, analysis and evaluation process

Have we identified operations linked to our Significant Environmental Aspects, Compliance Obligations and Environmental Objectives? If not, how will this be done?

What processes do we have to evaluate compliance with our Environmental Obligations? Is this process effective?

What type of monitoring, measurement, analysis and evaluation do we need to ensure that:

i) we are complying with applicable Compliance Obligations?

ii) Operational Controls are being implemented correctly?

iii) we are achieving our Environmental Objectives?

How do we identify the equipment used for any of the monitoring or measurement listed above?

How do we ensure that monitoring and measurement equipment is properly calibrated and maintained?

Our next step on monitoring, measurement, analysis and evaluation is to...

> *Resource 39 EMS Program Measurement Criteria Worksheet*
>
> *For each of the following EMS components, describe the component's objectives, activity measurements, results indicators and review period:*
>
> - *Communication Plan*
> - *Stakeholder input*
> - *EMS training*
> - *Review of Aspects*
> - *Operational Controls*
> - *Environmental Review of New Processes*
> - *Setting Environmental Objectives*
> - *Environmental Management Program*
> - *Documentation*
> - *Regulatory Compliance and other Obligations*
> - *Pollution Prevention*
> - *Who is an appropriate contact when work is completed?*

TRACKING EMS PERFORMANCE

To have a successful EMS it is important to determine criteria you can use to measure, and therefore monitor, the performance of the organization's Systems and Procedures. Determining such measurement criteria, (also known as key performance indicators), will help you evaluate the success of your overall EMS Program. Performance indicators therefore measure overall success.

When choosing what to monitor, consider adopting the concept of the 'vital few' — that is, choosing a limited number of factors that have a substantial impact on the outcome of the process upon which you are concentrating. The key thing to work out in doing this is to figure out what those factors are and how to measure them.

The most effective environmental monitoring and measurement systems use a combination of process and outcome measures. **Outcome measures** look at results of a process or activity such as the amount of waste generated or the number of spills that took place. **Process measures** look at the things that are used to do something such as the amount of paint used per unit of product or the number of employees trained on a topic. For best results, select a combination of process and outcome performance measures that are right for your organization.

When monitoring EMS performance there are several types of performance indicators that should be scrutinized. These are:

- Management performance indicators - These provide information on the organization's capabilities and efforts in managing areas such as training, resource allocation, purchasing and funding.
- Operational performance indicators - These provide information on the environmental performance of activities such as process inputs (quantity of materials processed and recycled, energy and water used), process outputs (waste, emissions, noise, heat and light), maintenance and emergency events.
- Safety indicators - such as the frequency of injuries and their seriousness.
- Customer-related indicators - such as complaints and delivery targets met.
- Production indicators - such as amount produced, cost and stock levels.
- Human resources indicators - such as training days provided per employee and staff turnover rates.

- Financial performance indicators - such as the amount of available working capital.

The following are examples of EMS performance indicators for your EMS that can be tracked over time:

- Number of Significant Environmental Aspects included in the Environmental Program.
- Number of Environmental Objectives met.
- Amount of hazardous waste generated per unit of production.
- Employee sick leave absences and their working environment.
- Percentage of employees completing environmental training.
- Average time for resolving corrective action.
- Energy or water use per unit of production.
- Percentage of solid waste recycled and reused.
- Number of complaints received and the number of responses made to such complaints.
- Number of pollution prevention ideas generated by employees.
- Resources used per unit of product or service.
- Pollution (by type) generated per unit of product or service.
- Number of products that have a recycling program.
- Number of non-compliances.

The results shown by these environmental performance indicators will become the basis of your future plans and for documenting continuous improvement. The purpose of these indicators is however different from the specific measurement criteria you developed for evaluating progress toward individual Objectives. The performance indicators focus on how well the overall System for improving Environmental Management is functioning. Therefore select performance indicators that will help you and other employees decide whether success has been achieved or whether improvements in the Procedures need to be made.

You will need performance indicators that describe how well the Environmental Policy is being implemented. In addition you will need performance indicators for all of the other components of your EMS. The measurement criteria selected for each component of your EMS (for example communication, documentation, and stakeholder outreach and training programs) will probably be significantly different. One approach is to measure actions. For example the number of:

- Meetings held with stakeholders;
- Documented Information created;
- Employees trained; and
- Hours of training.

Carrying out an action however, does not always mean that the expected results will always follow. For example providing training won't always change people's behaviour. Consider the objective of each EMS component and define a way to measure results so that you are satisfied that the Objectives are actually being achieved.

MEASURING IMPROVED POLLUTION PREVENTION

Measuring pollution prevention achievements is part of tracking performance but may be different from, and often more difficult than, measuring environmental achievements in general. For example, measuring the reduction in a waste stream might only mean that the waste has been transferred to another medium and so is not reduced. It is therefore important to measure the reduction at the source of waste generation. It is also important to measure activities that your organization directs towards pollution prevention and so sources of information such as permit applications, purchasing information, utility bills, hazardous waste manifests and Material Safety Data Sheets can be analyzed to help track pollution prevention. In addition, administrative Procedures can be established to support pollution prevention activities. For example, Procedures in each organizational area for identifying pollution prevention opportunities could be established, as could having a chemical or raw material inventory system.

CALIBRATING EQUIPMENT

A part of monitoring and measurement activities is ensuring that all equipment used within the organization is correctly calibrated. To do this, firstly identify all significant process equipment and activities that directly affect your environmental performance. As a starting point look at those key process characteristics you identified earlier. You can then measure the equipment itself (for example by measuring the paint flow rate through a flow gun to see if it is within the optimal range for transfer efficiency) or you can add measurement equipment to a process to help measure its important characteristics (for example by placing a thermometer on a plating bath to ensure that the temperature is kept within an optimal range which then cuts the need for re-plating and the creation of waste product).

Some organizations place environmentally-critical monitoring equipment within a special Calibration and Preventive Maintenance Program. This helps to ensure more accurate monitoring and makes employees aware of which instruments are most critical.

ENERGY CASE STUDY

Day-to-day business operations such as purchasing, using energy and handling materials need to be planned and continuously monitored in order to understand if the organization's Systems are functioning correctly. If not, remedial action should be taken before things get out of control. A good example is energy use. Energy is vital to every organization. Without energy there would be no heating, cooling, lighting nor movement of goods and people. Also from an Environmental Manager's point of view energy use and its reduction is usually one of the easiest areas of an organization to target in order to make some positive environmental benefits and financial cost savings. In order to do this firstly identify the quantity and cost of energy supplied and used by the organization. Find out if utilities are being purchased effectively. Utility invoices for fuel, electricity and water, as well as site energy Documented Information and sub-metering accounts, for at least one year should be carefully checked. This enables you to evaluate where energy is being used, how much and in what form. Take a UK-based office environment as an example. The amount of energy used within the office is predictable and so can be controlled. The air temperature should be around a comfortable working temperature of 18°C to 21°C. Therefore heating or air conditioning will probably be required at times to maintain levels of thermal comfort. This should be a controlled and monitored process – i.e. when the temperature reaches the required levels then heating or cooling is no longer required and should automatically cease until the time when the temperature falls below, or rises above, the desired temperature range. At this point the heating or cooling system should then start once again.

SPACE-HEATING ENERGY MONITORING AND CONTROL

Taking the UK as a typical country located in the northern hemisphere - during the heating season (which is usually from September to May), the weather conditions change quite dramatically. Bear these external factors in mind, but also realise that for comfort healthy people require an air temperature of at least 18°C (or 21°C for the elderly, very young or where there are ill people). Some people will start to feel too hot if the temperature rises above about 24°C. This of course depends upon factors such as what people are doing, their age and what they are wearing. In the organization there may be a requirement for specific temperatures for specific processes, such as in a factory handling chocolate or where there are chilled produce such as in a wholesale cut-flower warehouse.

The energy used for space heating varies with external temperature – as the temperature outside falls, more heating energy is required to maintain the temperature inside the building. Therefore heating a room should be a controlled process. Allowing the internal temperature of a building to fall below, or go above, comfortable levels is not satisfactory as productivity will decrease and eventually lead to ill-health.

The daily difference in temperature between the required inside temperature and the 24-hour mean outside temperature when the required inside temperature is higher than the maximum daily outside temperature is measured in degree days – see Figure 14.

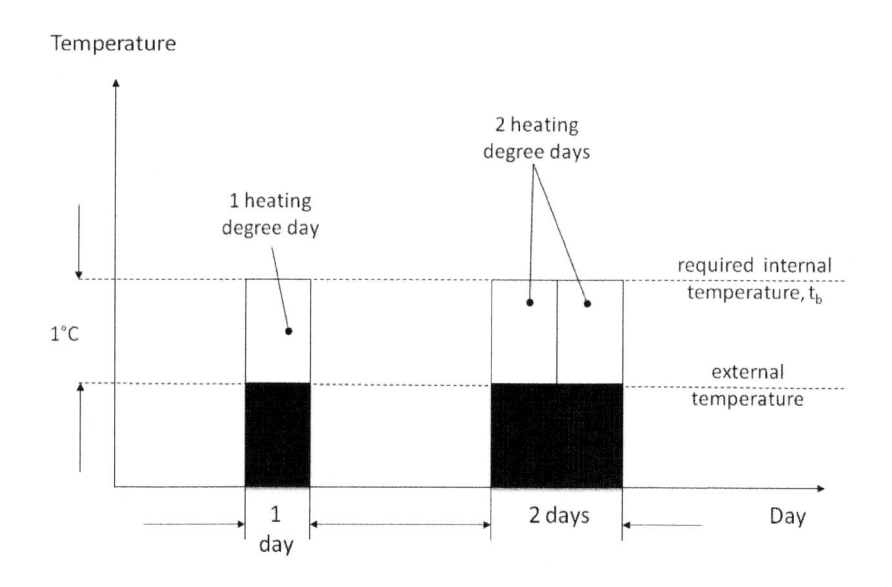

Figure 14 Schematic diagram of heating degree days example

The required internal temperature t_b, is the temperature above which no space heating is required. For the UK, t_b = 15.5°C as usually inside a building there will be sources of heat, called internal heat gains, such as machinery, appliances such as computers, TVs and fridges, as well as human inhabitants.

Predicting energy demand is therefore possible for space heating (as it relies upon the external air temperature). It is also possible to predict the amount of energy used to heat water (which may for example, depend upon work patterns) and the energy used for process needs (which may vary with the level of process output).

Predicting energy use can be achieved by following these steps:

STEP 1: Obtain energy use data for at least one year from energy invoices for all fuels used within the organization such as gas, coal and wood as well as for electricity. Annual fuel bills give a fair sense of how energy use changes over time. For example space heating is seasonal and so will typically be used less in the UK in summer and more in the winter.

STEP 2: Summarise and tabulate the data that was collected in step 1. This will provide insights into the trends and patterns of energy use within the organization. By converting all energy use into common standardized units (which are Joules, signified by 'J', for energy) a clearer picture will emerge about the types of energy sources being used and which are most costly in terms of monetary value and environmental cost. Resource 40 provides an example of how this can be done. The proportions of each energy type can now be found.

In this example most (83%) of the energy used was purchased in the form of oil – which is an environmentally polluting fossil fuel. However in terms of the cost of the energy supplied most (57%) of the money spent was used to buy electricity. Therefore if money saving was of prime importance then the amount of electricity should be reduced, not oil as oil is relatively cheap per Joule. However if the cost divided by the amount of energy delivered (in Joules) is calculated to indicate the cost efficiency of money spent with respect to the amount of energy delivered the highest by more than 3 times is electricity. This indicates that electricity should be the target of at least the initial round of energy efficiency measures.

> *Resource 40 Example energy data*
>
> **Electricity**: 902500 kWh = 3249GJ and represents 14% of total energy used. It cost £37400 which represents 57% of the total cost of energy used or £11.5 for every GJ
>
> **Gas**: 5500 therms = 580GJ and represents 3% of total energy used. It cost £1880 which represents 3% of the total cost of energy used or £3.2 for every GJ
>
> **Oil**: 440000 litres = 18480GJ and represents 83% of total energy used. It cost £26200 which represents 40% of the total cost of energy used or £1.4 for every GJ

STEP 3: Analyze more detailed energy data, ideally data that spans a whole year as this will include energy used for heating and cooling and will highlight seasonal trends. Ideally energy consumption and cost data will be available to you on a monthly basis. If so, this level of data will make is easier to spot trends and patterns that occur over time. Using the data obtained, a graph of energy use for each month can be plotted. An example is shown in Figure 15.

If trends are noted in the data then explanations should be sought for them. In Figure 15 for example, less energy is used during the warmer summer months than in the winter. This implies that at least some of the energy is used for heating and probably also lighting as both lighting and heating is needed less during the summer. Of note also is the energy consumption figure for August which seems uncharacteristically high than similar months. This may indicate that something out of the ordinary happened with respect to energy consumption during this month. Or perhaps the energy data is erroneous for August? Whichever is correct, further and better informed, targeted investigations are now possible.

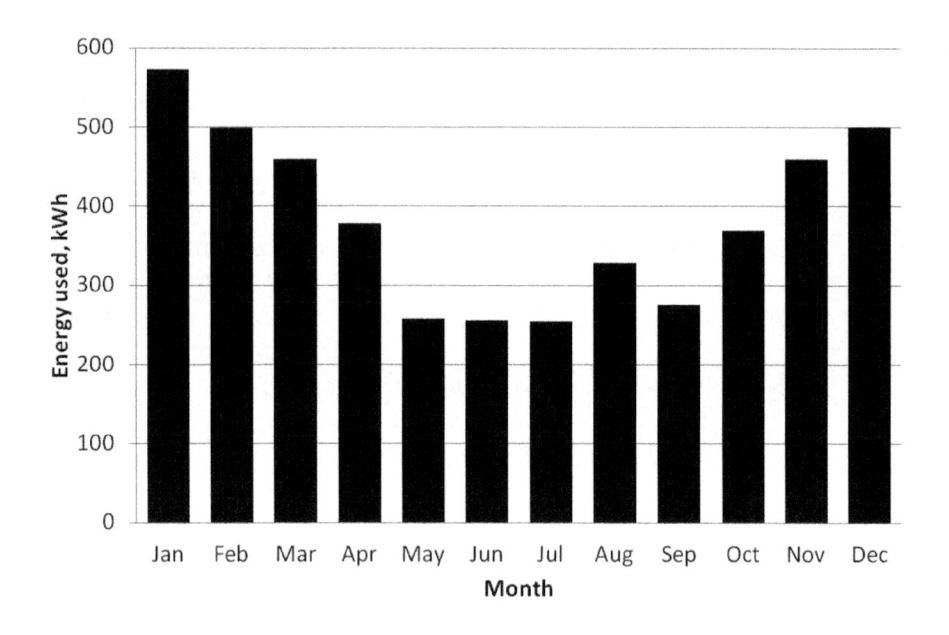

Figure 15 Graph of monthly energy consumption data

A seasonal or cyclical pattern in the monthly energy consumption data suggests energy is being used for things that are linked to the season, such as heating and lighting. An upward or downward trend reflects changes in energy demand, energy efficiency or perhaps changes in operating practices which are irrespective of season. A lack of a clear link between energy use and the time of the year suggests a lack of control over how energy is consumed throughout the year. There will typically also be a steady base load whereby a constant amount of energy is used throughout the year. This can be the case for example, when a heating system serves a variety of purposes such as for space heating and hot water requirements. It is also useful to investigate the high and low values of energy consumption, as these could indicate excessive energy use or system-shut down periods or there could be anomalies caused by mistyping or misreading data values.

Such a simplistic approach as that described above is not wholly satisfactory as it could be that some months saw typically unseasonal weather and so the energy required would be abnormally high or low. One way to account for the changes in the weather is to use degree days as a 'normalized performance indicator'. This simply means that variations in performance due to a change variable, in this example the weather (indicated by using degree days), can be taken into consideration without skewing the results. Data can be normalized not only to consider variations in weather, but can also be used for comparisons with other factors that may be important to you such as geographical locations, hours of use, number of staff or floor area of your premises. Which performance indicator is used will be determined by understanding what energy use is mostly dependent upon and what you want to compare it with. What is important is that energy use is corrected for the effects of changes in the chosen dependent variable.

For the example data shown in Figure 15, the dependent variable is outside air temperature and so degree days can be used as the dependent variable to normalize the energy consumption data. In this case degree data for the specific (or nearest) location under investigation is required. This data is then tabulated and degree day (as the independent variable) and energy consumption (as the dependent variable) data is plotted.

The resulting graph (Figure 16) is the energy signature for the building under investigation using the energy consumption data used in Figure 15.

The energy signature now shows a strong trend in the plotted data – in this case the data can be approximated to the general form of a straight line. This is now more useful as we can now predict how energy use will change with degree day values which are directly linked to the weather. In this case the equation for a straight line is in the general form . . .

$$y = mx + c$$

... where x and y are the variables on the horizontal and vertical axes respectively, m is the slope of the line and c is the intercept where the line cuts the y axis, i.e. when x = 0. This can also be thought of as ...

Energy use = (slope of line x degree days) + intercept

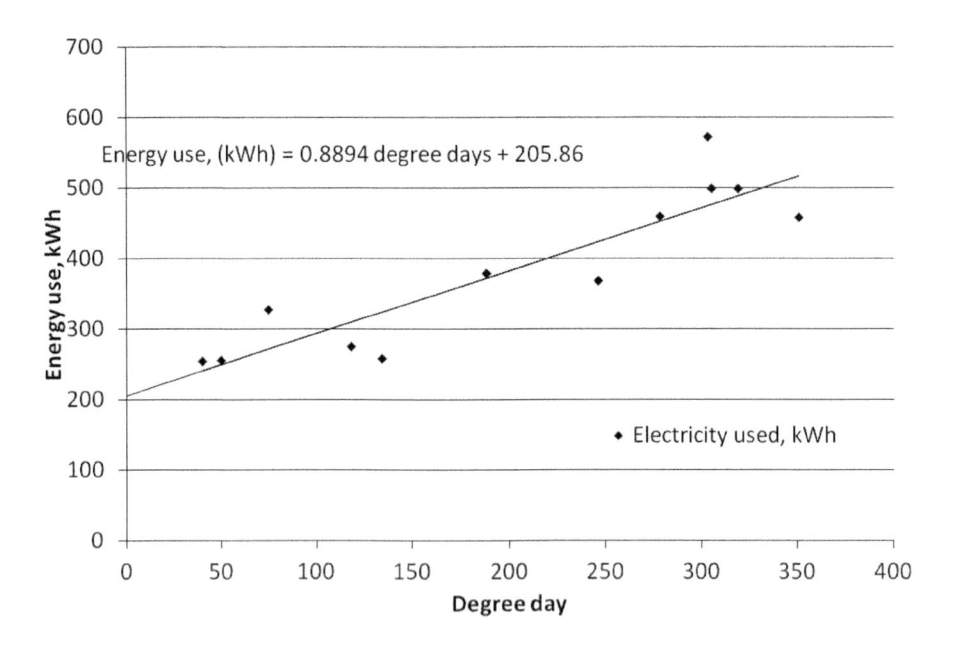

Figure 16 Example energy signature

The intercept indicates the level of energy that is consumed regardless of the degree day, and in this case is termed the base load. The amount of energy used above the base load is that energy that is used because of the degree day value, i.e. due to changes in the outside air temperature. This can be calculated by multiplying the slope of the line, m, with the degree day value, x.

The energy signature now reveals useful information about how energy is being used. The base load indicates which proportion of energy is independent of degree days and so in this example has probably little to do with space heating or lighting.

The distance the energy data points are away from the best fitting straight line through all the data points also indicates the level of control that exists over energy used for space heating and lighting with respect to the external air temperature. If there is good control of these systems, through the proper use of room thermostats for example, the distance the data points are away from the straight line will be small. By installing energy efficiency measures that target space heating and lighting, the variable portion of the total energy used will be reduced. However such measures will not affect the base load as energy use contributing to the base load is independent of the weather and change in the degree day value. Energy efficiency measures targeted at reducing the base load energy consumption will cut the base load and so will also reduce the total amount of energy used.

Armed with an energy signature for a building the next part of an energy analysis is to identify opportunities for other improvements. Now focus can move to the building fabric to make it more energy efficient and to appliances used within the building that consume energy. Each building is different and so some detective work may be required.

Undertaking a detailed energy analysis in this way can provide a detailed picture about how energy is used within the building by providing things such as lighting, space heating, refrigeration and other processes. This then also enables the installation of energy efficiency improvement measures to be prioritized by tackling the biggest energy consumers first.

INTERNAL AUDIT

Internal audits are undertaken by colleagues from within a different part of your organization and act as a 'dress rehearsal' to help you get things right before the external auditor starts work.

Once an EMS is established it is crucial to assess whether the System is suitable and to ensure that planned arrangements for the EMS are being followed. It is relatively easy to create a System that works well in the absence of change; the more difficult challenge is to have in place a System that meets its EMS requirements when faced with real-life, dynamic and changing business conditions. Auditing your EMS is a way to check if the EMS is being used as it was intended and so EMS audits are pivotal to maintaining a viable System - especially in the face of accidents, emergencies, changing circumstances, staff turnover and other organizational changes.

EMS auditing is a systematic and recorded way to verify that an EMS is functioning properly. More specifically, audits are used to objectively obtain and evaluate evidence to determine whether an organization's EMS conforms to EMS criteria and to communicate the results of this check to the EMS owners. There are two broad categories of audit:

1) Data gathering – in which the main objective is to establish baseline information such as during Environmental Reviews or in the case of site or packaging audits; and
2) Verification audits which aim to verify the EMS is complying with defined requirements such as during regulatory compliance audits.

So the purpose of environmental audits can vary from a check to ensure legal compliance, to an evaluation of if the organization is achieving its Environmental Objectives. Whilst they can be time-consuming EMS audits are critical to EMS effectiveness. The systematic identification and reporting of EMS deficiencies to managers provides a great opportunity to keep managers' focused upon the environment whilst also improving the EMS, its performance and the System's cost-effectiveness.

For an EMS Audit Program to be effective audit procedures and protocols need to be developed along with setting an appropriate audit frequency. To determine an appropriate EMS audit frequency consider the nature of the organization's operations along with its identified Significant Environmental Aspects and Impacts, the results of monitoring processes and previous audit findings. Usually all parts of the EMS should be audited at least annually. The entire EMS can be audited at one time or the organization can be split into discrete elements if more frequent audits are required. Sometimes more frequent audits are beneficial – especially if there have been incidents of poor environmental performance or if the organization is about to seek external accreditation for its EMS. Audit procedures therefore should describe audit planning, its scope, frequency and methods. They should also describe the key responsibilities and the reporting mechanisms for the audits. Then auditors can be selected and trained. Ensure also that audit Documented Information are kept safe.

By necessity audits are a sampling exercise as auditors probably can't spend enough time to cover the whole organization and all its processes. As audits have to be systematic, formal and independent so as to avoid biased results auditors have to look for evidence about environmental performance which is objective, verifiable, documented and unaffected by emotion or prejudice. Sources of evidence useful to auditors are most typically interviews and informal questions asked of staff, a review of relevant Documented Information and observations made on a tour of the site.

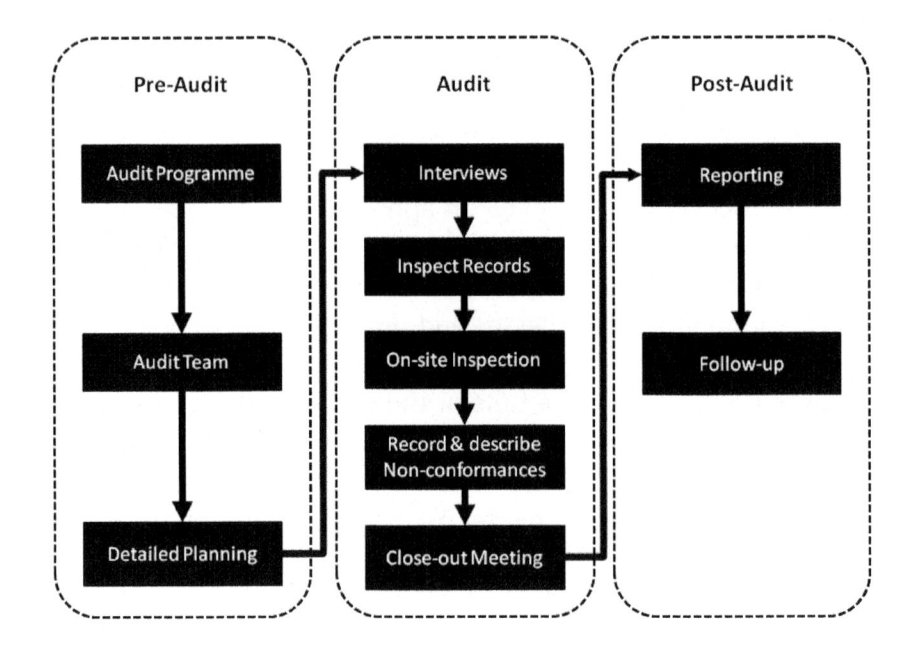

Figure 17 Phases of an Environmental Management System audit

Figure 17 shows the three generalized phases of an EMS audit. The phase before the on-site audit itself is undertaken is concerned with planning for the audit and ensuring that audit staff have the right experience and qualifications for them to undertake a satisfactory audit. In this phase, the audit scope and objectives are defined. A lead auditor can delegate audit responsibilities to fellow team members (if there is an audit team). An audit agenda and plan is also developed and a thorough review of all related Documented Information undertaken at this stage. The documents requested by the Auditor(s) from the organization for this stage of the audit usually includes the Environmental Policy, the results of any Environmental Reviews and the Environmental Manual. Details of relevant Compliance Obligations and authorizations will also probably be required. A pre-audit questionnaire may be sent to the organization a few weeks before the site visit which is designed to collect data useful in discovering general information about the organization (such as staff numbers and organizational hierarchy), relevant legal consents and permits that the organization has; a site plan so the site visit can be organized efficiently; process diagrams of the processes under scrutiny and requests for access into any appropriate restricted areas during the audit. Following this 'desk-based' study an audit protocol and appropriate checklists are drafted and passed to the organization to allow them time to organize access to the required areas and information before arrival of the audit staff. Sometimes audits are conducted without such notification being given, especially where there has been a recent and serious accident, emergency or pollution incident.

The on-site audit starts with an opening meeting in which the auditors and the organization's staff confirm the scope and objectives of the audit, its timetable and details of interviews, Documented Information required and physical observations that need to be undertaken and the data that needs to be scrutinized. Auditors therefore need good interpersonal skills such as listening and managing interviews in a tactful way. When auditing care needs to be taken with any verbal or hearsay information offered from staff as sometimes those being asked answer with what they think the auditor wants to hear rather than with information regarding how things really are.

EMS auditor training should occur soon after the person has been appointed as an Auditor, but should also include ongoing training to ensure the skills and knowledge of the team is kept up-to-date. Commercial EMS auditor training is available but it might be more cost-effective to coordinate with other organizations in your area (perhaps through a trade association) to sponsor an auditor training course upon which all auditing staff can enrol. Familiarity with environmental regulations, organization operations and environmental science can be useful for auditors and in some cases may be essential to adequately assess the EMS. Some auditor training can also occur in the workplace. Your organization's first few internal EMS audits can be considered part of auditor training, as long as you ensure that an experienced auditor leads, or at least takes part in, such training. Auditors should also be independent of the activities being audited to ensure unbiased reporting of audit findings. This can be a challenge for small organizations as staff usually known most areas of the organization and so it is difficult for them to remain objective and unbiased in their views. If the organization has a Quality Management System in place consider using the organization's quality auditors as EMS auditors because whilst some additional training might be needed for EMS auditing many of the required skills are similar to both roles.

Staff should also ensure that any gaps or deficiencies in the System identified by auditors are corrected in a timely fashion and that the appropriate corrective actions that have been implemented are recorded. Staff undertaking a Management Review of the EMS can then use this valuable information as EMS audit results are useful in helping to identify trends or patterns in EMS deficiencies.

Resource 41 provides a checklist which you can use to develop an Audit Procedure.

Resource 41 Help in developing an organization's Audit Procedure

Focus the EMS audits on objective evidence of conformance with the Environmental Management System.

During an audit, auditors should resist the temptation to evaluate for example, why a Procedure was not followed — that step comes later.

Ensure that auditors review all identified deficiencies during the audit with people who work in the relevant areas. This will help the auditors verify that their audit findings are correct whilst also reinforcing employee awareness of EMS requirements.

If possible, train at least two people as internal auditors. This will allow auditors to work as a team and will allow audits to take place when one auditor is unavailable.

Communicate the audit scope, criteria, schedule and other pertinent information to people who work in the affected areas before starting an audit. This helps to avoid confusion and facilitates the audit process.

Consider integrating the EMS with the regulatory compliance audit processes, but remember that these audit processes have different purposes.

While you might want to communicate the results of EMS audits widely within your organization, the results of compliance audits might need to be communicated in a more limited way.

An EMS audit is a check on how well the System meets established EMS requirements. An EMS audit is not an audit of how well employees do their jobs.

A 'Non-conformance' is the EMS term for something that is not working as described within the EMS. A non-conformance can be relatively serious or relatively minor. Serious issues are classed as 'Major Non-conformances' and less serious issues as 'Minor Non-conformances'.

The following phenomenon would be classed as Major Non-conformances:

- Failure to consider the Life Cycle Assessment of the organization's activities.
- A clause in the EMS which is not followed in practice.
- Total absence of a clause within the EMS.
- Failure to report a legal non-conformance.
- Consistent failure to respond to external communication.
- Failure to convert Environmental Objectives into the Environmental Management Program.
- Four minor non-conformances are equivalent to one major non-conformance.

Minor non-conformances include things like a slight discrepancy between procedural requirements and actual practice; a failure to keep, and be able to retrieve, environmental Documented Information and an isolated System lapse. An experienced auditor may also be able to make useful and helpful observations about a potential opportunity for Improvement if poor practice has been spotted.

Once the audit is complete, and within an Audit Team meeting, the auditors should discuss and agree their overall findings before holding a closing meeting with the people being audited. At the closing meeting the preliminary results of the audit will be delivered by the Lead Auditor, starting with thanks and gratitude shown to the organization under scrutiny and a summary statement which includes both good and bad examples of observed practice along with an outline of the observed non-conformances. This is usually followed by a discussion and agreement about the next steps (which should include a formal, written report and any follow-up actions as necessary).

Resource 42 provides questions, the answers to which can help you determine the organization's audit Procedure. A customizable example Procedure is shown in Appendix 16: Procedure for EMS and Regulatory and other Compliance Obligations Audits.

Resource 42 Questions, the answers to which can help you to determine your organization's audit Procedure

Have we developed an EMS Audit Program? If not, how will this be accomplished?

Who needs to be involved in the Audit Procedure?

Is there another audit program with which EMS Audits could be linked, for example our Quality Management System audits?

Have we determined an appropriate audit frequency? What is the basis for the existing frequency?

Should the frequency of audits be modified?

Have we selected EMS auditors?

What are the qualifications of our auditors?

What training has been conducted or is planned for our EMS auditors?

Have we conducted EMS Audits as described in the Audit Program? Where are the results of such Audits described? How is the Documented Information of these Audits maintained?

How are the results of EMS Audits communicated to senior managers?

Our next step on EMS Audits is to...

MANAGEMENT REVIEW

An EMS must be reviewed periodically to stay relevant and useful. Such Management Reviews are critical to continual improvement and to ensure that the EMS will continue to meet the organization's needs as time goes by. You can therefore use Management Reviews to assess how changing circumstances might influence the suitability, effectiveness or adequacy of the EMS. Changing circumstances might be internal to the organization (such as new raw materials, changes in products or services, new customers, etc.) or might be external factors (such as new laws, new scientific information or changes in adjacent land use). To do this your organization's senior managers should review and evaluate the EMS at scheduled time intervals. The goal of the Review should be to allow managers to bring about overall System and organizational improvements. The specific scope and frequency of the Review therefore depends upon the size and complexity of the organization but should include the elements shown in Figure 18.

The Management Review should be carried out by the level of management responsible for such elements as shown in Figure 18 as this will help ensure that appropriate actions are taken and adequate resources are available. Some organizations combine Reviews with other meetings, such as directors' meetings. Other organizations hold 'stand-alone' Reviews.

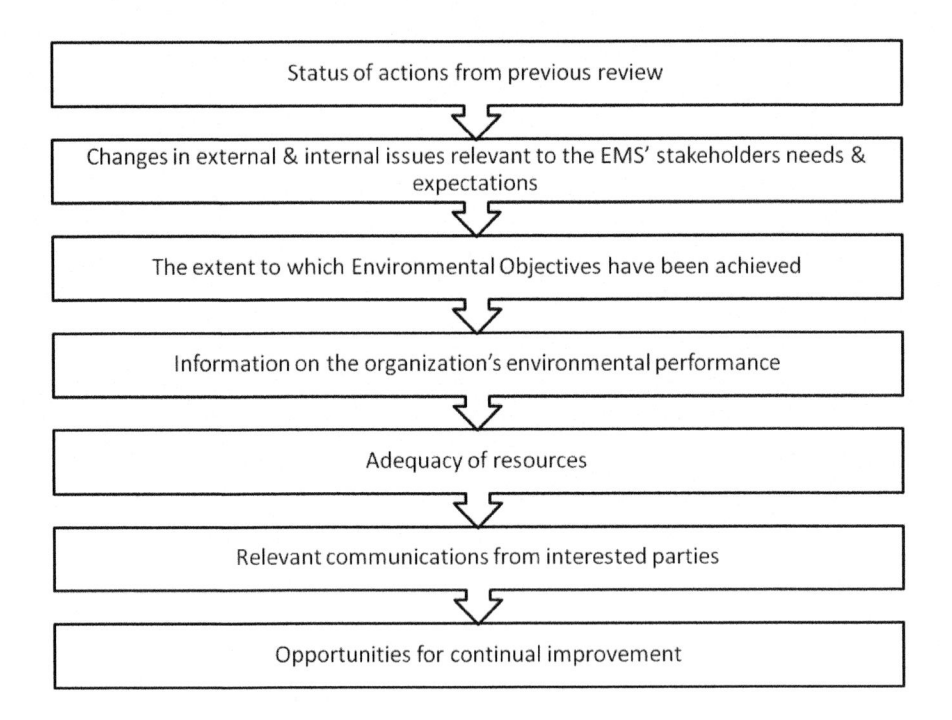

```
┌─────────────────────────────────────────────────────────────────┐
│           Status of actions from previous review                │
└─────────────────────────────────────────────────────────────────┘
                              ↓
┌─────────────────────────────────────────────────────────────────┐
│ Changes in external & internal issues relevant to the EMS'      │
│              stakeholders needs & expectations                   │
└─────────────────────────────────────────────────────────────────┘
                              ↓
┌─────────────────────────────────────────────────────────────────┐
│     The extent to which Environmental Objectives have been      │
│                            achieved                              │
└─────────────────────────────────────────────────────────────────┘
                              ↓
┌─────────────────────────────────────────────────────────────────┐
│      Information on the organization's environmental performance │
└─────────────────────────────────────────────────────────────────┘
                              ↓
┌─────────────────────────────────────────────────────────────────┐
│                     Adequacy of resources                        │
└─────────────────────────────────────────────────────────────────┘
                              ↓
┌─────────────────────────────────────────────────────────────────┐
│         Relevant communications from interested parties          │
└─────────────────────────────────────────────────────────────────┘
                              ↓
┌─────────────────────────────────────────────────────────────────┐
│              Opportunities for continual improvement             │
└─────────────────────────────────────────────────────────────────┘
```

Figure 18 Elements considered in the Management Review of an Environmental Management System

As a minimum consider conducting Management Reviews at least annually. At these meetings ensure that someone records what issues were discussed, the decisions made and what actions were agreed upon during Management Reviews as these will form part of the Documented Information for your EMS and should be kept as evidence of the Management Review's results. Resource 43 provides a checklist of things to consider when undertaking a Management Review.

> *Resource 43 Issues to consider when holding an EMS Management Review*
>
> *Is the Environmental Policy still relevant to what we do?*
>
> *Are environmental roles and responsibilities clear?*
>
> *Are we applying resources appropriately?*
>
> *Are we meeting our Compliance Obligations?*
>
> *Are the Environmental Procedures clear and adequate? Do we need others? Should we eliminate some?*
>
> *Have changes in processes had an effect upon the EMS?*
>
> *How effective are our measurement and assessment systems?*
>
> *Can we set new measurable performance objectives?*
>
> *Do changes in laws, regulations or other related Compliance Obligations require us to change our approaches?*
>
> *What stakeholder concerns have been raised since the last Review?*
>
> *Is there a better way?*
>
> *What else can we do to improve?*

What the outputs from a Management Review should be are shown in Figure 19.

Resource 43 Issues to consider when holding an EMS Management Review and Appendix 17: Procedure for EMS Management Review can help with this.

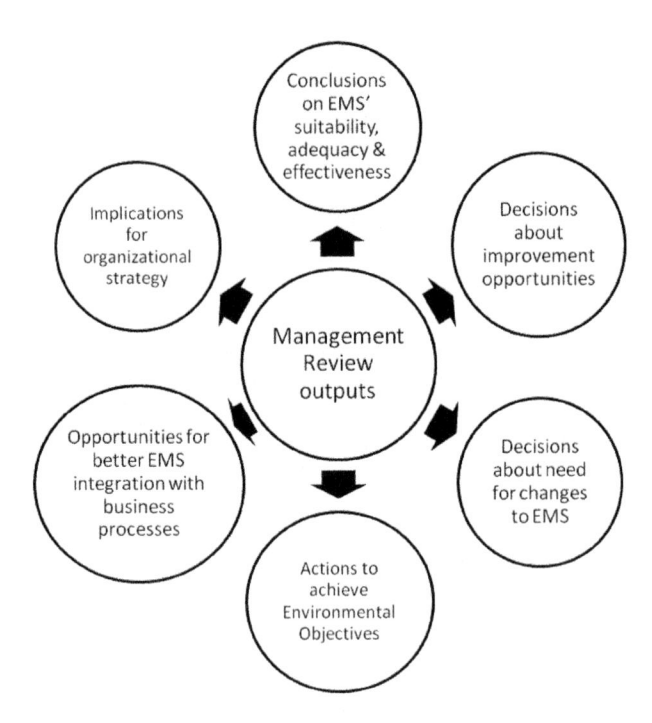

Figure 19 Management Review outputs

Management Reviews also offer opportunities to keep the EMS efficient and cost effective. If EMS procedures don't add value, eliminate them. A good way to do this is to involve people who have knowledge about the EMS and who can make decisions about the organization and its resources. Ensure too that the actions agreed upon in the Management Review are carried out.

Resource 44 EMS Management Review Record

EMS Management Review Record	
Date of Review meeting:	
People present at meeting	
Name	Job title
Conclusions:	
Actions to be taken & deadline	Person(s) responsible
Signed: Environmental Manager	Signed: Facility Manager
Revision date	**Description**	**Sections affected**

13   ACT PHASE: IMPROVEMENT

Improvements to your EMS can be made by considering what has happened to date, if there have been any problems, and what future actions need to be taken to avoid such actions from reoccurring. See Figure 20.

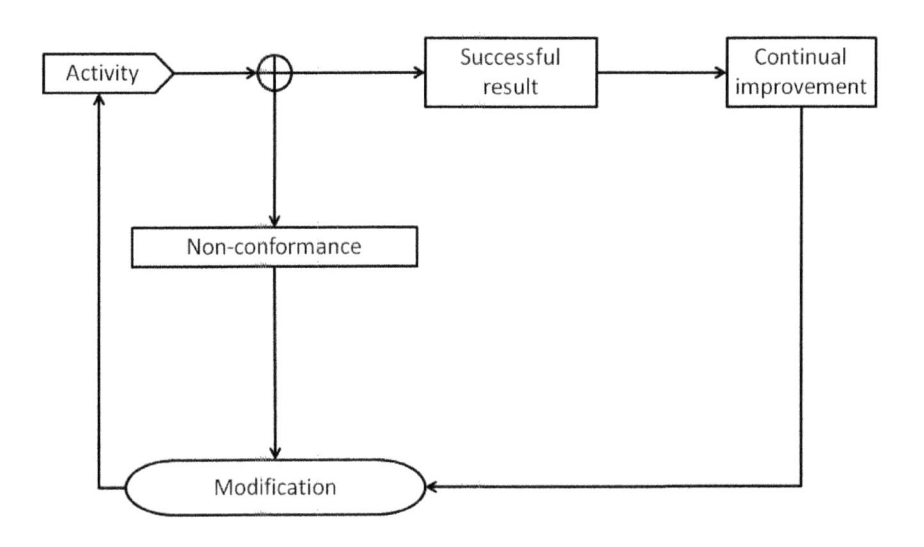

Figure 20 Continual improvement is the aim of every EMS

As part of the EMS, opportunities for improvement should be formally identified and the actions required to achieve the intended outcomes of your EMS should be put into place.

NON-CONFORMITY AND CORRECTIVE ACTION

No EMS is perfect. You will probably identify problems with your System (especially in the early phases) through audits, measurement or in other ways. The EMS will also need to change as the organization adapts and grows. So to deal effectively with such System deficiencies your organization needs to establish a Procedure to ensure that such problems are identified and the root causes of the problems are investigated and remedied. Once the cause or causes of problems are known corrective actions can be put into place. Once all of this has been done to ensure satisfactory Systems are in place, the actions should be tracked and their effectiveness verified. All EMS nonconformities and any other System deficiencies should be analyzed to detect patterns or trends arising in their cause(s). This will allow you to anticipate and prevent similar problems from occurring in the future, as this approach is generally cheaper than fixing problems after they occur.

There are five corrective actions that the organization needs to implement when nonconformity exists, as shown in Figure 21.

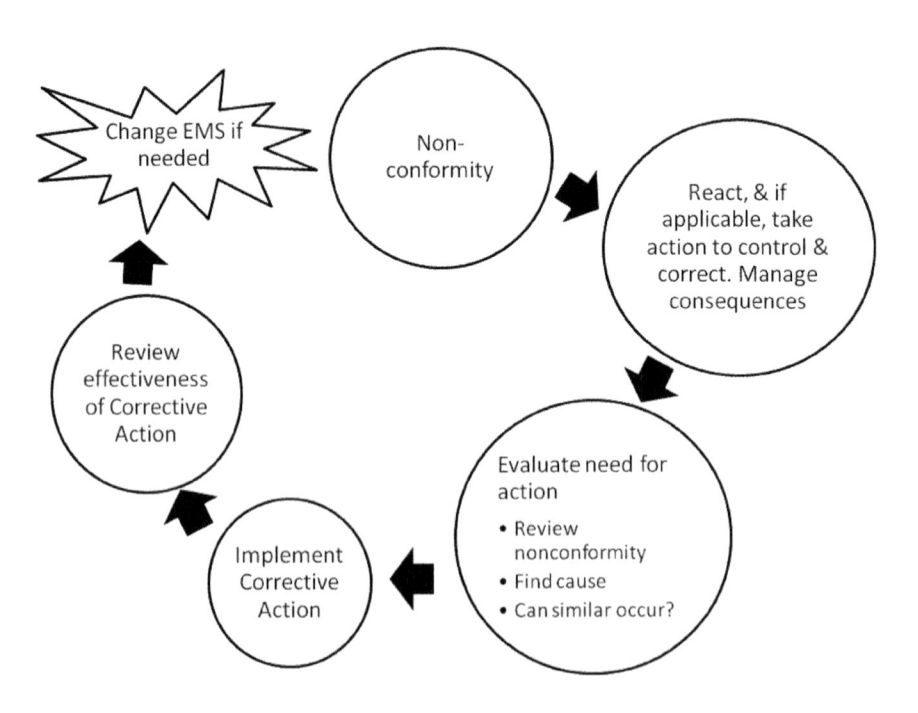

Figure 21 Nonconformities and Corrective Actions required

FINDING CAUSES OF PROBLEMS

You will need to establish a way to find why the organization is failing to conform to the EMS. In some cases the cause may be obvious and in others, obscure.

EMS problems usually happen because of:

- Poor communication.
- Faulty or missing Procedures.
- Equipment malfunctions.
- Lack of proper maintenance.
- Lack of training.
- Lack of understanding of Compliance Obligations.
- Failure to enforce the appropriate rules.
- Corrective Actions are established and put in place but the actions fail to address the root cause(s) of problems.

Root cause analysis is a way to identify causes of problems and then determine associated preventive actions that could be taken to improve matters. For example, if a spill occurs several times in your raw material transfer area you would attempt to identify why the spills are occurring so that you could address the cause and so prevent future spills. Creating a root cause diagram helps you organize your thoughts when you analyze the organization's potential for creating Environmental Impacts. An example is shown in Figure 22 which shows some factors which could have contributed to a milk spill which caused some fish deaths in a nearby river. In the figure, a diagonal line represents the main component that potentially caused the spill whilst a horizontal line represents an important element potentially contributing to the cause of the spill.

This analysis can be done by one person or by a group with one person recording the ideas produced. Each diagonal line represents a main component of the process which resulted in an Environmental Impact. Each horizontal line stemming from the diagonal represents an element which contributes to that component. For example milk is delivered to an on-site canteen but some milk is accidently dropped and the spilt milk runs into a nearby river and kills fish. A factor that could have contributed to that accident and the Environmental Impact of dead fish is the level of awareness in the delivery person that spilt milk could cause such an Environmental Impact and what that person should do in that situation to avoid such an Impact.

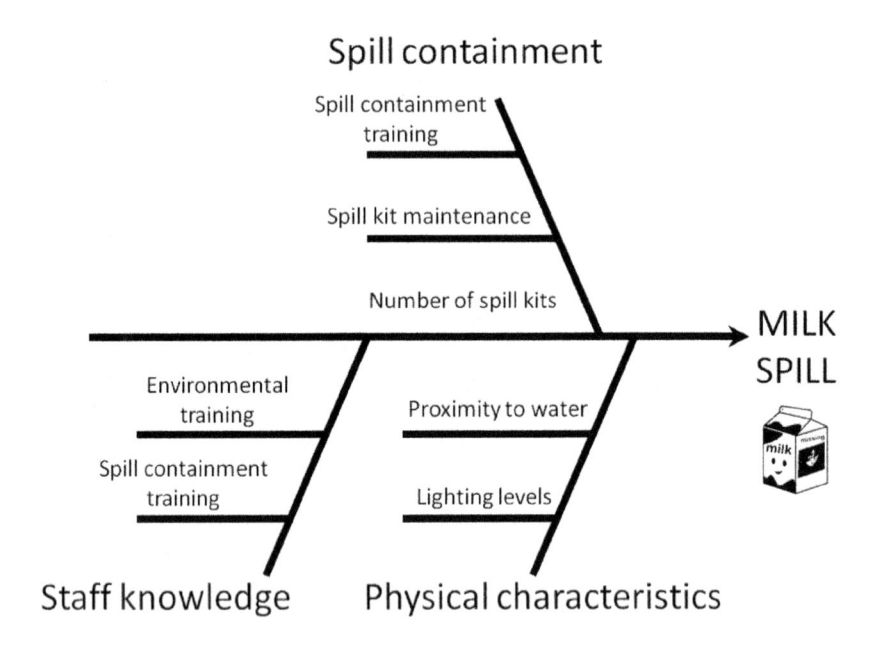

Figure 22 Root cause diagram for a milk spill which enabled milk to get into a nearby river, killing some fish

TAKING CORRECTIVE ACTION

Once you are aware of a problem that is impeding your organization's ability to meet its Environmental Objectives, you must resolve it and take action as quickly as possible. Make sure that staff responsibilities for remedial actions and remedial work schedules are clear so that Corrective Actions occur in a timely manner. In other cases employees may recognize the need for Corrective Action and provide their own good ideas for solving problems, so find ways to get them involved in this improvement process - for example via suggestion boxes, contests or incentive programs. Initially most EMS problems may be identified by internal auditors. However, over the long run, many problems and good ideas for improvements may be identified by other staff. This should be encouraged.

It's important to determine whether a lapse in the System is temporary or due to some flaw in Procedures or control measures. For this reason communicate the findings of such investigations to employees and provide follow-up training for changes in the Procedures that may then be required.

If your organization has a Quality Management System you can use the Corrective Action Procedures as a model for the EMS Corrective Action Procedure. Also try to combine some elements of your Management Review and Corrective Action processes if you can. Organizations that do this use part of their Management Review meetings to review nonconformities, discuss causes and trends, identify Corrective Actions and assign responsibilities. Try however to avoid being too bureaucratic — simple methods often work quite effectively. The amount of planning and documentation needed for Corrective Actions will vary with the severity of the problem and its potential Environmental Impacts.

Ensure that the Corrective Action Procedure specifies responsibilities and time schedules for completion. Once you spot a problem the organization must be committed to resolving it in a timely manner and so it is necessary to review your progress to ensure that effective actions are being, or have been, taken. But make sure such actions are based on good information and analysis of causes or else the intended consequences may not materialize. Corrective Actions should of course resolve the problem they are targeting. You can then consider whether the same or similar problems exist elsewhere in the organization and prevent the problem from recurring.

Use your answers to the questions provided in Resource 45 to help determine your organization's Corrective Action Procedure, a customizable example of which is given in Appendix 15: Procedure for Corrective Action.

CONTINUAL IMPROVEMENT

In the true spirit of the 'Plan, Do, Check, Act' model which is embedded within the International Environmental Management Systems standard ISO 14001, your EMS needs to be continually improved to ensure that the environmental performance of your organization becomes increasingly better. This includes the EMS's suitability, adequacy and effectiveness.

Resource 45 Questions, answers to which help develop your organization's Corrective Action Procedure

Do we have an existing Procedure for Corrective Action? If yes, does that Procedure need to be revised? In what way? Who needs to be involved in this Procedure?

How are nonconformities and other potential System deficiencies identified?

How do we determine the causes of System deficiencies? How is this information used?

How do we track the status of our Corrective Actions and how can information on non-conformities and Corrective Actions be used within the EMS?

How do we ensure the effectiveness of our Corrective Actions?

Our next step on Corrective Action is to...

14 WORKS CITED

British Standards Institute, 2015. *BS EN ISO 14001:2015 Environmental management systems - requirements with guidance for use,* London: British Standards Institute.

15 INDEX

A

Annex SL, 13
Audit, 13, 82, 120, 121, 122, 123, 124, 125, 126, 127, 128, 148, 149, 168, 187, 189, 191, 192, 193, 195
Awareness, 8, 10, 52, 59, 60, 61, 125, 138, 162, 163, 164, 175, 192

C

Calibrating, 111
Commitment, 21
Communication, 10, 66, 67, 70, 75, 83, 87, 107, 146, 153, 164, 165
Competence, 10, 14, 60, 87, 146, 161, 162, 195
Compliance Obligations, 5, 10, 14
Context, 14, 17, 21, 35, 41, 48, 52, 61, 79, 84
Continual improvement, 11, 135, 140
Corporate Social Responsibility, 4, 6, 19
Corrective action, 11, 14, 82, 83, 87, 96, 97, 109, 135, 138, 139, 140, 148, 164, 168, 187, 189, 191, 192
Cross Functional Team, 16, 23, 24, 27, 32, 33, 98, 151, 158, 164, 165, 171, 175, 185

D

Degree days, 113, 117, 118, 119
Document, 11, 83, 85, 86, 87, 147, 165, 170, 172
Document control, 11
Documented Information, 5, 10, 76, 154, 155, 162, 172, 176, 179, 193, 196

E

Emergency preparedness, 11, 96
EMS leaders, 23
EMS team, 32, 33, 35
Energy, 3, 109, 111, 118, 119, 183
Energy signature, 117, 118, 119
Environmental Action Plan, 55, 56, 57
Environmental Aspects, 10, 14, 19, 28, 29, 32, 33, 36, 45, 46, 47, 51, 52, 53, 56, 60, 61, 82, 83, 87, 89, 90, 92, 93, 105, 106, 109, 121, 145, 151, 155, 157, 158, 163, 164, 165, 166, 167, 175, 187, 195
Environmental impacts, 1, 4, 7, 8, 14, 35, 60, 98, 148
Environmental Management Program, 10, 14, 82, 87, 107, 126
Environmental Management Representative, 15, 23, 27, 31, 32, 33, 145, 147, 149, 151, 153, 157, 161, 164, 165, 171, 175, 177, 186, 189, 192, 195
Environmental Objectives, 10, 27, 28, 36, 41, 42, 47, 49, 51, 52, 53, 55, 57, 82, 89, 92, 95, 96, 104, 106, 107, 109, 120, 126, 138, 145, 155, 166, 177, 196
Environmental Policy, 10, 11, 17, 18, 21, 33, 35, 36, 37, 38, 39, 41, 51, 52, 53, 57, 60, 61, 77, 82, 89, 91, 110, 122, 131, 145, 146, 151, 163, 164, 165, 166, 167, 177, 178, 179, 181, 195, 196
External temperature, 112

H

Holistic approach, 14, 89

I

Initial Environmental Review, 24, 25
Integrating systems, 13, 21
ISO 14001, 3, 4, 5, 7, 13, 18, 140, 151, 153, 155, 161, 163, 165, 169, 171, 175, 177, 185, 187, 189, 191, 195

L

Leadership, 5, 9, 14, 21
Legislation, 1, 37, 47, 145, 148, 165, 177, 181
Life cycle, 4, 5, 14, 18, 36, 38, 45, 46, 89, 90
Linear equation (y = mx + c), 117

M

Management Review, 11, 14, 83, 87, 105, 124, 129, 130, 131, 132, 133, 139, 149, 155, 193, 195
Measurement, 11, 103, 104, 105, 106, 107, 108, 109, 110, 111, 131, 135, 187
Monitoring, 11, 14, 87, 103, 104, 105, 148, 187, 196

N

Non-conformance, 14, 126, 148, 196
Normalized performance indicator, 117

O

Operational planning and control, 11, 89
Outsourcing, 17

P

Performance evaluation, 9, 103
Performance indicators, 64, 94, 105, 107, 108, 109, 110
Plan, Do, Check, Act, 1, 2, 3, 7, 8, 140
Pollution prevention, 18, 29, 39, 104, 109, 110, 111, 151

Q

Quality Management System, 13, 24, 81, 124, 128, 139

R

Regulatory agencies, 14, 42, 43, 147, 151, 153, 157, 164
Responsibility matrix, 29, 30
Risks, 10, 41, 42, 49, 54, 55, 79, 97
Root cause analysis, 137

S

Stakeholders, 6, 7, 14, 35, 36, 41, 48, 52, 53, 66, 67, 68, 69, 70, 71, 72, 73, 74, 80, 110, 163
Sub-contractors, 17, 68, 92, 175, 177

T

Training, 14, 24, 60, 61, 62, 64, 65, 82, 83, 87, 95, 100, 101, 146, 155, 161, 166, 183, 195

16 Appendix 1: Initial Environmental Review Assessment Checklist

This checklist can help as a useful starting point to check if your organization has any existing Systems in place which could be used in your EMS, as well as to help you identify where System development is required.

Structure and Responsibility
Organization has defined the roles, responsibilities and authorities to facilitate an effective EMS.
An Environmental Management Representative (EMR) has been appointed with defined roles and responsibilities to implement the EMS.
EMR reports on the performance of the EMS to senior managers for review and continuous improvement.
Environmental Policy
Senior staff have defined an Environmental Policy.
Policy is specific to organization and is appropriate to the nature, scale and Environmental Impacts of its activities, products or services.
Policy includes a commitment to continuous improvement in environmental performance and the prevention of pollution.
Policy includes a commitment to sharing information on EMS performance with the community.
Policy includes a commitment to comply with relevant environmental legislation and regulations.
Policy includes a commitment to meeting other requirements to which the organization subscribes.
Policy provides the framework for setting and reviewing Environmental Objectives and Targets.
Policy is implemented and maintained; communicated to all employees and made available to the public
Legal and Other Compliance Obligations
Organization has a Procedure to identify and access Compliance Obligations.
Organization maintains access to all current regulations.
Environmental Aspects
Organization has established and maintains a procedure to identify the Environmental Aspects that it can control or over which it can have an influence to determine those that have or can have Significant Environmental Impacts.

In its Significant Environmental Aspect determination organization has considered the Aspects associated with on-site contractor activities.
Significant Environmental Aspects form the basis for establishing process and management controls, environmental improvement programs and Significant Environmental Aspects for further investigation.
Objectives
Organization has considered technological options, financial, operational and business requirements in establishing its Objectives.
Organization has considering Compliance Obligations in establishing Objectives.
Organization has considered the views of interested parties in establishing Objectives.
Organization Objectives are consistent with Environmental Policy and its commitment to prevention of pollution.
Environmental Management Programs
Organization has established and maintained Environmental Management Programs that includes the means and time-frame for achieving its Objectives.
New activities, products or services are reviewed for potential Environmental Management Programs, plans and controls.
Organization has defined roles and responsibilities for the Environmental Review of new projects.
Project originator reviews and characterizes the environmental and energy aspects of a new project.
Training, Awareness, and Competence
The organization has performed a comprehensive environmental training and competence needs analysis.
Personnel whose work may create a significant impact or is associated with an Significant Environmental Aspect have received appropriate training.
Organization has a Procedure to make its employees aware of the importance of conformance with Policy and Procedures, the significant impacts associated with their work and their roles and responsibilities as these affect the Environmental Policy
Organization has a Procedure to make its employees aware of: requirements of the EMS, the consequences of departure from operating Procedures and Emergency Preparedness and Response Procedures.
Organization personnel performing tasks that can cause Significant Environmental Impact are competent based upon education, training and experience.
Communication
Organization has a Procedure for communication within the organization.
Internal communications Procedures are used to facilitate implementation of regulatory, organization policy and other requirements.
Organization has a Procedure to log external communications and record the responses to external communications that concern environmental issues.

Environmental Management Representative or designee responds to inquiries from the community and regulatory agencies.

A designated person, in consultation with the Environmental Management Representative, is responsible for responding to media communications.

Where the external communication relates to an environmental incident, appropriate Emergency Response Procedures are identified and followed. The organization has considered processes for informal communication of its SEAs and recorded its decision.

EMS Documented Information

Organization has information to describe the core elements of the EMS and their interactions.

Organization has information to provide direction to related documentation.

Document Control

Organization has a Procedure for controlling all Documented Information required by the EMS.

Authorized personnel review Documented Information for adequacy before use or release.

The Environmental Management Representative or designee maintains a master list of Documented Information.

Relevant Documented Information is available at the locations where they are needed. Obsolete Documented Information is removed from use or otherwise assured against unintended use.

Obsolete Documented Information retained for legal or preservation purposes are properly identified.

Organization has Procedure for defining responsibility concerning Documented Information creation/ modification.

Documentation is legible, dated and readily identifiable, maintained and retained.

Operational Control

Organization has identified operations with Significant Environmental Impacts.

Organization has planned maintenance activities.

Operations associated with Significant Environmental Impacts have Procedures to cover situations where their absence could lead to deviations from the Policy, Objectives and Targets.

Procedures stipulate operating conditions.

Organization has a Procedure related to the identifiable Significant Environmental Impacts of goods and services provided by contractors. It then communicates these to suppliers and contractors.

Organization communicates relevant organization-specific Environmental Procedures, work practices and requirements to contractors before work starts.

Emergency Preparedness and Response

Potential Environmental incidents and emergencies have been identified.

Methods for preventing, mitigating and responding to likely events that require an

emergency response have been established and maintained at the organization and involve the appropriate response personnel.
Roles and responsibilities for emergency communications within the organization have been established and are maintained.
The Emergency Preparedness and Response Procedures at the organization are reviewed and revised on an annual basis.
The organization emergency response leader records information necessary to determine corrective actions and any improvements to existing procedures that may be needed.
Monitoring and Measurement
Organization has Procedures for monitoring and measuring key characteristics of operations with Significant Environmental Impacts.
Organization has established metrics to track performance, relevant operational controls and conformance with Objectives.
Monitoring and measuring equipment is calibrated and maintained as shown in appropriate Documented Information.
Organization has documented procedures for periodically evaluating compliance with relevant environmental legislation and regulations.
EMR or designee is responsible for planning, scheduling and implementing internal environmental regulatory compliance assessments, including the identification of required resources.
The assessment team records audit information and issues a Corrective Action Notice when appropriate. Upon completion of Corrective Actions, the responsible person furnishes the EMR with a signed Corrective Action Notice.
Non-conformance and Corrective Action
Organization has a Procedure for non-conformance and corrective actions defining responsibility and authority for investigating and mitigating environmental impacts.
Each work team within the organization is responsible for identifying ways to: identify the root cause(s); take appropriate action; verify effectiveness and prevent recurrence on Non-Conformances.
Organization records and makes changes in Procedures resulting from performance feedback from corrective actions.
Documented Information
Organization has Procedure to identify, maintain and dispose of environmental Documented Information.
Each person responsible for maintaining a record has the responsibility for establishing the method for filing and indexing the Documented Information for accessibility.
EMS Audits
An audit program and procedure exists.
An EMS audit team will be formed whose membership has no responsibility within

the area to be audited.
An EMS audit schedule will be developed for each activity to be audited. Audit frequency is determined on priority basis that considers previous audit results and the environmental importance of the activity.
The EMS audit team has established a checklist of questions relating to the EMS. These questions are reviewed and amended as necessary based on audit findings and other factors.
During the audit the EMS audit team records audit observations, indicating items checked, individuals interviewed, any concerns identified and corrective or preventive actions completed during the audit.
The audit team records its findings.
The area representatives address the corrective and preventive action sections within on time and return the information to the audit team and the Environmental Management Representative.
The Environmental Management Representative notifies managers of likely regulatory non-compliance.
The audit team reviews corrective actions and confirms proper implementation either by a subsequent check or during the next audit.
Management Review
Management Reviews are conducted by the Environmental Management Representative and a management committee.
The Environmental Management Representative schedules Reviews regularly.
The Management Review addresses the need for changes to policy, objectives and other elements of the EMS, in light of EMS audit results.

17 Appendix 2: Procedure for Identification of Compliance Obligations

Purpose

[Organization's Name] is committed to complying with all relevant environmental regulations. It will also strive to meet other obligations made in its Environmental Policy such as commitments to community involvement, pollution prevention and continuous improvement. This Procedure describes how **[Organization's Name]** identifies relevant Compliance Obligations.

Activities Affected

EMS Coordinator

Forms Used

Resource 46 Legal and Compliance Obligations identification

References

Governmental/commercially-available publications

Other requirements to which **[Organization's Name]** subscribes

ISO 14001: clause 6.1.3.

Exclusions

None

Procedure

The Environmental Management Representative is responsible for tracking relevant environmental laws and regulations and evaluating their potential impact on the organization's operations. He or she employs several techniques to track, identify, and evaluate applicable laws and regulations. These techniques include commercial databases, trade association information, direct communication with national and state regulatory agencies and periodic refresher training on environmental laws.

As necessary, the Environmental Management Representative may call upon off-site resources such as consultants or attorneys.

The Environmental Management Representative compiles and maintains updated copies of applicable environmental laws and regulations.

The Environmental Management Representative, working with the EMS Coordinator and Cross Functional Team, correlates these regulations to the business activities and the related Environmental Aspects.

FREQUENCY

Ongoing

DOCUMENTED INFORMATION

A form for Compliance Obligations is maintained by the EMS Coordinator. The EMR maintains copies of the applicable Obligations.

RECORD OF REVISIONS

Describe the revision made, the date of the change and the sections of the Procedure affected.

Resource 46 Legal and Compliance Obligations identification

Purpose

*The **[Organization's name]** has developed this form to identify legal and other Compliance Obligations. The completed, updated Form will be maintained electronically by the Environmental Manager at **[location]**.*

Regulatory & Other Compliance Obligations

Obligation; Organization; Location; Expiration; Contact

Record Keeping Requirements

Records; Organization; Frequency; Location; Retention

Inspections Requirements

Audit Issue; Organization; Frequency; Location; Retention

Revision History

Revision Date & number; Revision details; Prepared by

18   Appendix 3: Procedure for Obtaining Agency Approval

Purpose

This Procedure describes the method to be implemented to secure approval from regulatory agencies for processes and activities at **[Organization's Name]** affecting air emissions, waste management or water discharges, as well as the method for other environmental approvals.

Activities Affected

All areas and departments

Forms Used

None

References

Appendix 2: Procedure for Identification of Compliance Obligations

Appendix 8: Procedure for Communicating With Stakeholders

Appendix 10: Procedure for Environmental Documented Information

ISO 14001: clause 8.1 and 9.1

Exclusions

None

Procedure

Where operations are identified as potentially requiring environmental permits, the EMS Coordinator shall coordinate the investigation and permitting process through the use of an informal 'permit team' comprised of (at least) the EMS Coordinator and, as appropriate, a representative from **[Organization's Name]** function responsible for the operation concerned.

All communications in connection with permits, and specifically those with the relevant regulatory agencies, shall be undertaken in conformance with the Procedure for Communication with Stakeholders.

The permit team shall develop a strategy to secure permits concurrently with existing operational timing plans. The Environmental Management Representative is responsible for communication of the issues to the Organization Management Team.

The EMS Coordinator shall coordinate the preparation, submission and negotiation of permit applications, operating through the permit team. Permits obtained shall be reviewed to ensure that they adequately cover the operation(s) concerned.

The permit team will review the terms and conditions in new permits and modify or establish operational controls necessary to ensure compliance with the permit.

FREQUENCY

Ongoing

DOCUMENTED INFORMATION

Documented information shall be retained consistent with the Procedure for Environmental Documented Information.

RECORD OF REVISIONS

Describe the revision made, the date of the change and the sections of the Procedure affected.

19 Appendix 4: Procedure for Environmental Aspects, Objectives, and Action Plans

Purpose

This Procedure defines **[Organization's Name]**'s method for the identification of Environmental Aspects of its operations and the determination of Significance for Aspects that have actual or potential Significant Impacts on the environment.

Activities Affected

All areas and departments

Forms Used

Identification and Significance Determination of Environmental Aspects - See Resource 12 Example Environmental Risk Assessment matrix

Setting Objectives – See Resource 13 Example Environmental Objectives and an Action Plan to achieve them

Environmental Training and Competence – See Resource 16 Training Needs Analysis — Environmental Courses; and Resource 17 Training Needs Analysis — Procedures by area or department

References

Appendix 1: Initial Environmental Review Assessment Checklist

Appendix 2: Procedure for Identification of Compliance Obligations

Appendix 8: Procedure for Communicating With Stakeholders

Appendix 13: Procedure for Emergency Preparedness and Response

Appendix 14: Procedure for Monitoring, Measurement, Analysis and Evaluation

ISO 14001: clause 6.1.2 and 6.2

Frequency

Ongoing

Documented Information

Documents shall be retained consistent with the Procedure for Environmental Documented Information.

Record of Revisions

Describe the revision made, the date of the change and the sections of the Procedure affected.

20 APPENDIX 5: PROCEDURE FOR ENVIRONMENTAL REVIEW FOR NEW PURCHASES, PROCESSES AND PRODUCTS

PURPOSE

This Procedure defines the method for identifying and evaluating the environmental issues of new projects at **[Organization's Name]** to:

a) Ensure that appropriate consideration is given to environmental issues prior to project approval and funding.

b) Ensure that new Environmental Aspects generated by projects are identified and their significance evaluated.

c) Provide a mechanism for the amendment of Environmental Management System elements and Action Plans to ensure that the EMS applies to such projects.

ACTIVITIES AFFECTED

All areas and departments

REFERENCES

Appendix 4: Procedure for Environmental Aspects, Objectives, and Action Plans

Appendix 6: Environmental Impact Assessment Evaluation Checklist

PROCEDURE

Areas and departments initiate Project Appropriation Requests when the need for project funding becomes apparent.

The initiating person or team shall identify and evaluate environmental issues associated with the project. A summary of this evaluation shall be recorded on the Project Environmental Checklist and added to the Appropriation Request. This process may be undertaken in liaison with the EMS Coordinator at the discretion of the initiating person or team, and shall include an identification of Environmental Aspects and Compliance Obligations for obtaining approvals from environmental regulatory agencies.

The initiating person or team shall submit the Appropriation Request and completed Project Environmental Checklist for review to the Environmental Management Representative (EMR).

The EMR shall review the proposed project to ensure that all relevant environmental issues have been identified and if incomplete, shall return the Appropriation Request and Project Environmental Checklist to the initiating person or team for alteration.

The EMR shall review the Environmental Aspects of the project, considering their significance.

Following appropriate review the EMR may approve the project by returning the Appropriation Request to the initiating person or team for further processing. If a project is not acceptable, the initiating person or team will coordinate any necessary actions to satisfy concerns identified. The initiating person or team in conjunction with the EMR, or designee, will coordinate any necessary prevention, mitigation or control activities associated with the project.

Environmental Aspects associated with projects shall be evaluated for environmental significance by the Cross Functional Team in line with the Procedure for Environmental Aspects, Objectives and Programs.

Changes to the EMS resulting from an Environmental Review of a project will be approved by senior managers.

Frequency

Ongoing

Documented Information

Documents shall be retained consistent with your Procedure for Environmental Documented Information.

Record of Revisions

Describe the revision made, the date of the change and the sections of the Procedure affected.

21 Appendix 6: Environmental Impact Assessment Evaluation Checklist

This checklist is a good starting point to help you assess the Environmental Impacts of newly proposed products, services, systems or processes. Add or remove issues as appropriate to your organization. Categorize the issues into the following categories: **Adequately covered; Not adequately covered;** or not currently appropriate.

Purpose and Need
Clear description of underlying need for the proposed project, as well as the purpose of proposed Project

Project Alternatives
Consideration of all relevant alternative types as well as alternative sites; alternative designs; alternative controls; structural alternatives; and non-structural alternatives. Including:

Description of all alternative actions or projects that are being considered and should include details about the:

a) Size and location of facilities
b) Land requirements
c) Operation and management requirements
d) Auxiliary structures
e) Construction schedules
f) Description of initial environmental impact assessment processes and results

Description of Environmental Setting
This should contain a definition of the region of concern, including boundary areas as well as details about the physical-chemical environment, such as:

a) Air resources such as meteorological data (e.g., temperature, wind); ambient air quality (e.g., particulates, ozone); and mobile sources of emissions (e.g., cars and truck).
b) Water resources such as:
   - surface water - location and type (e.g., estuaries, streams, lakes, and their position relative to the site); water quality information (e.g., dissolved oxygen, temperature, nutrients); existing pollutant sources (location and amount of discharges); future uses and a discussion of flooding events.

- ground water - description of key factors (e.g., depth to water table, overlying soils, geologic features); and water quality information (e.g., pH, solids).

c) Soils and geology including topography; soil structure; ground water movement; erosion potential; subsidence; seismic activity (e.g., proximity to faults, history of earthquakes and volcanic eruptions); and mineral resources (e.g., locations of deposits, types and quantities, ownership of mining rights).

Biological conditions such also be considered, such as:

a) Wildlife and vegetation including a description and listing of aquatic, wetland, and terrestrial flora and fauna (e.g., species lists, abundances); native species of wildlife and vegetation present; particularly invasive exotic species of wildlife and vegetation; and rare and threatened species.

b) Community and habitat characterization including maps and descriptions of the aquatic, wetland, and terrestrial communities found in and around the project site.

c) Ecologically Significant Features including support of broader ecosystems by the project site (e.g., if located along a flyway or other biological corridor); important ecological functions of the project site (e.g., nutrient source through flooding, storm water retention); characterization of relevant disturbance regimes, natural and project-induced (e.g., floods, fire, potential impact of logging); description of hydrologic processes (e.g., ground and surface water flows and durations); and description of important biotic interactions (e.g., interdependence of plants and animals at the site and with other sites).

Waste management and pollution prevention issues should also be considered including:

a) Locations of expected waste disposal or discharge.

b) Description of waste management techniques (e.g., treatment, storage, transport, recycling).

c) Projected waste characteristics (e.g., types, quantities, toxicity)

The socioeconomic environment will also be considered, including:

a) Land Use – a description of present and historic land use and a map of present and historic land use.

b) Population and housing - demographic information (e.g., average household size, age, age/sex distributions, and community cohesion).

Add or remove issues that are appropriate to your organization

22 APPENDIX 7: PROCEDURE FOR ENVIRONMENTAL COMPETENCE

PURPOSE

This procedure defines the process for identifying and planning environmental competence at **[Organization's Name]**.

ACTIVITIES AFFECTED

All areas and departments

FORMS USED

Resource 16 Training Needs Analysis — Environmental Courses

Resource 17 Training Needs Analysis — Procedures by area or department

REFERENCES

Appendix 2: Procedure for Identification of Compliance Obligations

Appendix 4: Procedure for Environmental Aspects, Objectives, and Action Plans

Appendix 8: Procedure for Communicating With Stakeholders

ISO 14001: clause 7.2

EXCLUSIONS

None

PROCEDURE

Training

A Training and Competence Needs Analysis (TCNA) and training schedule shall be completed and maintained by the Training Department to identify the level of instruction needed by personnel whose jobs may affect environmental performance and impact upon Compliance Obligations. The needs analysis and training schedule shall be reviewed and updated where necessary, at least annually and when requested by the Environmental Management Representative in consultation with the Training Department to ensure its continuing adequacy.

Knowledgeable individuals with appropriate expertise and experience in: operational environmental management; relevant environmental obligations for environmental training and training provision at **[Organization's Name]** shall develop the TCNA.

New, part-time and transferred employees, as well as permanent on-site contractors, shall be included in the Environmental Competence Program.

The Training Department shall maintain records of each individual's environmental training.

Awareness Raising

Environmental awareness shall be implemented as specified in the Procedure for Environmental Competence.

Staff Competence

Employee competence relevant to the EMS is determined through applicable training and through observation of performance by the employee's supervisor.

Frequency

Ongoing

Documented Information

Documents shall be retained consistent with the Procedure for Environmental Documented Information.

Record of Revisions

Describe the revision made, the date of the change and the sections of the Procedure affected.

# 23 Appendix 8: Procedure for Communicating With Stakeholders

Purpose

This Procedure defines the process for Internal environmental communication and awareness within **[Organization's Name]**, as well as external environmental communication between **[Organization's Name]** and external stakeholders.

Activities Affected

All areas and departments

Forms Used

Resource 9 An example Environmental Policy

Resource 23 Record of External Stakeholder Communication

References

Appendix 2: Procedure for Identification of Compliance Obligations

Appendix 3: Procedure for Obtaining Agency Approval

Appendix 7: Procedure for Environmental Competence

Appendix 11: Procedure for Document Control

Appendix 12: Procedure for Contractors and Sub-contractors

Appendix 13: Procedure for Emergency Preparedness and Response

ISO 14001: clause 7.4.

Procedure

Internal Communications and Awareness raising

Internal environmental communications shall be implemented to ensure those personnel at each relevant level and function, are aware of the following:

- The Environmental Management System.
- The importance of conformance with the Environmental Policy, and the EMS.
- The potential consequences of system non-conformances.
- Individual roles and responsibilities in achieving conformance with Procedures.
- The Significant Environmental Aspects associated with work activities and the environmental benefits of improved personal performance.

Internal environmental communications may be accomplished by the use of:

- Notice boards.
- Appropriate awareness training of personnel.
- Newsletters.
- Intranet and web-based notices.
- Team meetings and meeting minutes.
- Management Reviews.
- Corrective Action Requests.

Communication of environmental issues from employees to senior managers shall be handled by the Cross Functional Team member representing the affected area, in coordination with the Environmental Management Representative, (EMR). These communications shall be recorded.

Communication of changes to Compliance Obligations to employees shall be handled by the Area or Department Manager. These communications shall be recorded.

External Communications

External communications concerning the Environmental Aspects of the organization should be directed to the Security Manager, Human Resources Manager or the Environmental Management Representative.

The EMR or EMS Coordinator is responsible for responding to inquiries from interested parties and regulatory agencies. These will be recorded on Resource 23 Record of External Stakeholder Communication. The Human Resources Manager or designee is responsible for sending current copies of the Environmental Policy to interested parties.

The Human Resources Manager in consultation with the EMR responsible for responding to media communications. When community concerns relate to an environmental emergency, the Procedure for Emergency Preparedness (see Appendix 13: Procedure for Emergency Preparedness and Response) shall be consulted. The EMR is responsible for determining the need for, and preparation of, any notification to regulatory agencies as required.

Frequency

Ongoing

Documented Information

Documents shall be retained consistent with the Procedure for Environmental Documented Information.

Record of Revisions

Describe the revision made, the date of the change and the sections of the Procedure affected.

24 Appendix 9: EMS Manual

A suggested structure for an EMS Manual is described below.

Purpose

This Manual defines the scope of **[Organization Name's]**'s Environmental Management System (EMS) and provides links between System documents and ISO 14001.

Scope

[Organization Name]'s EMS provides a mechanism for Environmental Management throughout all departments. The Environmental Management System is designed to cover Environmental Aspects that the organization can control and directly manage and those it cannot control or directly manage but over which it can be expected to have an influence.

Issue and Update

The control of this Manual is in accordance with **[Organization Name]**'s Procedure for Environmental Document Control. All copies of this Manual not marked 'CONTROLLED DOCUMENT' are uncontrolled and should be used for reference purposes only.

Amendments to this Manual will be issued by the Environmental Management Representative (EMR) following approval by the Organization Manager.

Environmental Policy

The **[Organization Name]** Environmental Policy is endorsed by the Organization Manager. The policy covers all activities at the organization. The Policy includes a commitment to continual improvement and prevention of pollution as well as a commitment to meet or exceed relevant environmental legislation, regulations and other Compliance Obligations. The Policy will be reviewed annually by senior managers, communicated to all employees, and made available to the public in accordance with the Environmental Communication Procedure.

Environmental Aspects

[Organization Name]'s Cross Functional Team (CFT) identifies the Environmental Aspects that the organization controls and over which it may be expected to have an influence and determines which of those Aspects are considered significant. Discussions regarding significance are recorded in CFT meeting minutes. These aspects are reviewed at least semi-annually by the CFT or when there is a new or changed process or activity at the organization. The EMR maintains CFT meeting minutes and other relevant information.

COMPLIANCE OBLIGATIONS

[Organization Name] has established an Environmental Procedure for the purpose of identifying, accessing and communicating Compliance Obligations that are applicable to the organization. Additional information is also available through legal publications. Local regulations are identified, accessed and communicated by the EMS Coordinator. At least annually, the EMS Coordinator will review the most current national, regional, provincial, state and local Compliance Obligations as applicable to **[Organization Name]**.

ENVIRONMENTAL OBJECTIVES

The CFT has developed Objectives and an Action Plan for each Significant Environmental Aspect. These Objectives and Plan define:

1. The performance objectives (Investigate, Control, Maintain or Improve) for each Significant Environmental Aspect.

2. The specific, quantified actions that define those performance objectives.

3. The planned deadlines for the achievement of the Actions.

Objectives are developed considering Significant Environmental Aspects; technological options; financial and operational plans and stakeholder views.

ENVIRONMENTAL ACTION PLANS

The CFT establishes Environmental Management Programs (EMPs) as a means to achieve Environmental Objectives. These Programs define the principal actions to be taken, those responsible for undertaking those actions and the scheduled times for their implementation. The EMPs are developed by the CFT and approved by senior managers.

ORGANIZATIONAL STRUCTURE AND RESPONSIBILITY

EMS roles, responsibilities and authorities are defined at relevant functions and levels within the organization. Senior managers provide the resources for the implementation and control of the EMS, including: training, human resources, financial resources, and technical and information services. The EMR has primary responsibility for establishing, operating and maintaining the EMS. A CFT provides routine EMS support and reports directly to the EMR.

TRAINING, AWARENESS AND COMPETENCE

[Organization Name] identifies plans, monitors and records training needs for personnel whose work may have a Significant Impact upon the environment. It has an Environmental Procedure to train staff so they are aware of the Environmental Policy, SEAs, their roles and responsibilities in achieving conformance with the Policy and Procedures and with the requirements of the EMS. The Training Coordinator is responsible for maintaining employee training records. Appropriate Documented Information are monitored and reviewed on a scheduled basis. Staff competency is determined by the employee's supervisor.

COMMUNICATION

[Organization Name] has established and will maintain a Procedure for internal and external communications regarding Environmental Aspects and the EMS.

EMS DOCUMENTATION

This Manual identifies all Documented Information relevant to the EMS. A copy of EMS Documented Information can be obtained from the EMR.

DOCUMENT CONTROL

[Organization Name] has established an Environmental Procedure for controlling all Documented Information related to the EMS. This Procedure describes where Documented Information can be located and how and when it is reviewed. The Procedure ensures that current versions are available and that obsolete Documented Information is removed from use or are suitably identified. Controlled Documented Information are kept by the EMR.

OPERATIONAL CONTROL

The CFT is responsible for identifying operations and activities associated with Significant Environmental Aspects that require operational controls in Procedures, work practices or Environmental Management Programs. This Documented Information defines the mechanisms for the establishment, implementation and maintenance of the EMS and ensure that the system is maintained in accordance with the Environmental Policy and Objectives and is communicated to suppliers and contractors. System Procedures cover the management and control of both the EMS and the Significant Environmental Aspects that the System manages. These Procedures apply to the whole organization. Work Instructions cover the environmental control of specific operational activities.

EMERGENCY PREPAREDNESS AND RESPONSE

[Organization Name] has an Environmental Procedure to identify the potential for, and to respond to, accidents and emergency situations and for preventing and mitigating the Environmental Impacts that may be associated with them. Emergency methods are reviewed by the CFT on an annual basis and after the occurrence of accidents or emergency situations.

MONITORING AND MEASUREMENT

[Organization Name] has established an Environmental Procedure to monitor and measure the key characteristics of its operations and activities that can have a significant impact on the environment. This Procedure includes calibration and maintenance requirements and ensures that Documented Information will be retained.

[Organization Name] has established an Environmental Compliance Program which outlines the requirements to periodically review Compliance Obligations and report results to managers on a yearly basis.

Non-conformance and Corrective Action

[Organization Name] has an environmental Procedure for defining responsibility for handling and investigating non-conformances, for taking action to mitigate impacts and for initiating and completing corrective action. Any changes in Procedures resulting from corrective actions are implemented and recorded. The Audit Program Leader maintains the Documented Information.

Documented Information

[Organization Name] has a Procedure for identifying, maintaining and disposing of environmental Documented Information. The Documented Information includes training records and the results of audits and reviews. They are readily retrievable and protected against damage, deterioration and loss. The Areas and Departments maintain their own environmental Documented Information. Record and document retention is also specified in the Procedure.

Environmental Management System Audit

Periodic System audits are conducted to ensure that the EMS has been properly implemented and maintained. The results of these audits are provided to managers. Audits are performed according to a schedule that is based on the environmental importance of an activity, the results of previous audits, and the audit schedule. All auditors are trained and audit records are kept with the Audit Program Leader.

Management Review

Senior managers review all elements of the EMS annually to ensure its continuing suitability, adequacy and effectiveness. Meeting minutes record these reviews and are kept by the EMR.

Record of Revisions

Describe the revision made, the date of the change and the sections of the Procedure affected.

25 Appendix 10: Procedure for Environmental Documented Information

Purpose

This Procedure identifies the management of environmental Documented Information at **[Organization's Name]**.

Activities Affected

The areas and departments specified in the Index of Environmental Documented Information.

Forms Used

Index of Environmental Documented Information – See Resource 47 Example Index of Environmental Documented Information

Resource 23 Record of External Stakeholder Communication

Resource 24 Questions, answers to which help develop EMS documentation

Resource 25 Questions, answers to which will help you develop information you'll need to document as part of your EMS.

References

ISO 14001: clause 7.5.

Procedure

Documented Information shall be maintained and retained. Record retention will be consistent with applicable Compliance Obligations.

Each area or department manager shall have access to a master list of all EMS Documented Information relevant to their area or department.

Each team or individual responsible for maintaining a record has the responsibility for establishing the method for filing and indexing Documented Information to ensure accessibility.

General Rules

Documented Information shall be legible, easily retrievable and stored and maintained so as to prevent damage, deterioration or loss of the record.

Documented Information

Documented Information shall be retained as specified in this Procedure.

Record of Revisions

Describe the revision made, the date of the change and the sections of the Procedure affected.

Resource 47 Example Index of Environmental Documented Information

EMS Index - Document Control File

Environment Sustainability Policy

EMS Manual

Environmental Aspects Register

Detailed Environment & Sustainable Development Governance Structure

Legislation Register

Terms of Reference - Environment and Sustainable Development Governance Meetings

Biodiversity Policy

Use of Natural Resources – Environmental Management Procedure

Sustainable Procurement – Environmental Management Procedure

Land Development & Buildings – Environmental Management Procedure

Waste Management – Environmental Management Procedure

Travel/ Transport - Environmental Management Procedure

Training Needs Analysis

Pollution Prevention - Environmental Management Procedure

Environmental Management Action Plan

Communications Plan

Hazardous Waste Disposal Guide

Clinical/Offensive Waste Disposal Guide

Carbon Reduction Commitment

Reducing Paper Use

Site Induction – Contractors – Consultants

Socially Responsible Investment

Sustainable Business Travel and Hierarchy

Contractors – Waste Licences – Duty of Care Paperwork

Waste Transfer Note Template

Sustainability Considerations for Event Management

26 APPENDIX 11: PROCEDURE FOR DOCUMENT CONTROL

PURPOSE

This Procedure defines the mechanism for controlling Documented Information that is part of the EMS and so ensures that personnel requiring access to EMS documents have the most up-to-date versions and are aware of the document control process.

ACTIVITIES AFFECTED

All areas and departments

FORMS USED

Resource 23 Record of External Stakeholder Communication

Resource 24 Questions, answers to which help develop EMS documentation

Resource 25 Questions, answers to which will help you develop information you'll need to document as part of your EMS.

Master Document List – See Resource 48 Example Master documents list

REFERENCES

ISO 14001: clause 7.5.

PROCEDURE

The Environmental Management Representative (EMR) shall be responsible for coordinating, developing, issuing and controlling EMS Documented Information.

Procedures shall be in a format that is consistent with other controlled information at the organization.

The EMR shall maintain a master set of EMS documents.

Each area or department manager should maintain a list of, or have access to, all EMS documents relevant to their area or department.

Relevant documents are available at the locations where they are needed.

Personnel ensure current versions are available and used.

The Cross Functional Team shall review and approve changes to EMS Documented Information.

All controlled documents shall be marked with the words 'CONTROLLED DOCUMENT'.

Controlled versions of System documents may be placed on the computer system for access by area or department personnel.

All controlled documents issued by the EMR shall be recorded on a Master Document List.

The EMR shall provide notice to affected personnel to ensure that they are aware of the new or revised document, as well as issue controlled copies of those documents to appropriate personnel.

Frequency

All documents not marked with the words 'CONTROLLED DOCUMENT' shall be considered uncontrolled.

Documented Information

Documented information shall be retained consistent with the Procedure for Environmental Documented Information.

Record of Revisions

Describe the revision made, the date of the change and the sections of the Procedure affected.

Master Document List

For each document record the following:
- ID number
- Title
- Issue date
- Locations at which the document and any copies are kept and who authorized the original document.

Resource 48 Example Master documents list

EMS Manual

Environmental Procedures

Environmental Instructions

EMS Forms, Checklists and Guidelines

Objectives and Programmes

Register of Environmental Aspects

Registers of Compliance Obligations

External documents including legislation, professional guides and codes of practice.

27 Appendix 12: Procedure for Contractors and Sub-contractors

Purpose

This Procedure defines the process for controlling the Environmental Aspects of on-site contractors and their sub-contractors at **[Organization's Name]**.

Activities Affected

All areas and departments authorizing contractors to work on-site.

Forms Used

Resource 49 Example Contractor Environmental Briefing Statement

Resource 50 Contractor Work Method Statement

References

ISO 14001: clause 4.4.6

Exclusions

Contractor activities and services that are performed outside of the organization.

Contractors performing emergency services.

Contractors providing clerical, accounting or other similar administrative services

Procedure

A Cross Functional Team led by the Environmental Management Representative (EMR) develops a process to obtain and review contractor Method Statements.

The need for contractor services is identified and a request for a Method Statement is prepared by the initiating activity. Information related to contractor on-site activities shall be recorded by the contractor using a Contractor Method Statement. Completed Contractor Method Statement forms will be submitted to the initiating person or team. The EMR will evaluate Method Statements to identify potential environmental issues and concerns. Prior to on-site work contractors shall be provided with information and Documented Information to ensure their awareness of **[Organization's Name]**'s EMS and their conformance to it and submit a completed Contractor Method Statement to the initiating person or team. While on site, contractors shall conform to **[Organization's Name]**'s EMS and to all applicable Compliance Obligations. Contractors shall maintain appropriate Documented Information.

General Rules

Contractors shall ensure their staff are aware of **[Organization's Name]** requirements.

DOCUMENTED INFORMATION

Documents shall be retained consistent with the Environmental Documented information Procedure.

RECORD OF REVISIONS

Describe the revision made, the date of the change and the sections of the Procedure affected.

Resource 49 Example Contractor Environmental Briefing Statement

[Organization's Name]'s *Environmental Management System is designed to meet the requirements of ISO 14001 Standard. The principle elements of the EMS and Environmental Policy are to:*

- *Establish and operate effective Procedures aimed at controlling environmental performance to comply with all relevant environmental legislation and regulations.*

- *Set objectives aimed at achieving continual improvement in environmental performance.*

- *Introduce improvements that contribute to the prevention of the pollution at the source, where possible.*

An important part of the EMS relates to the control of contractors and their sub-contractors, who are required to comply with **[Organization's Name]**'s *Environmental Policies and Procedures. The nature of the contractor activities is such that contractor personnel have significant potential to affect the environmental performance and regulatory compliance of the organization. Contractor personnel and the organization must therefore work together to achieve the organization's Environmental Policy, the Environmental Objectives and the protection of the environment. Contractors must be aware of the importance of compliance with relevant environmental legislation and regulations and the consequences of non-compliance. The contractor is responsible for developing a Contractor Method Statement and returning it to* **[Organization Name]**'s *Environmental Management Representative. The contractor is responsible for communicating to all contractor personnel the information in their Method Statement as well as information from this Contractor Environmental Briefing.*

Contractor Personnel Environmental Information

All contractors working at *[Organization's Name]* are required to comply with the requirements of the EMS and the Environmental Policy. This Environmental Guide provides general details of the Environmental Management System and Environmental Policy.

Contractors working on-site

Contractors shall not allow discharges to drains or sewers without prior approval from the EMS Coordinator. Contractors shall provide adequate spill prevention for all bulk materials.

Contractors shall immediately notify *[Organization's Name]*'s Safety Committee Champion and the Project Manager of any spills, releases or other environmental incidents.

Contractors shall immediately notify the EMS Coordinator and the Project Manager of any abnormal conditions found during excavation at the organization. Visibly discolored soils, soils with a discernible odor or heavily stained concrete must not be removed from the site without prior approval of the EMS Coordinator.

Contractors shall properly label, store and dispose of all waste materials generated from their activities in line with *[Organization's Name]*'s Procedures or guidance.

If *[Organization's Name]*'s personnel are required to work with potentially hazardous materials brought on-site by a contractor, prior approval of the material by the EMS Coordinator is required. Contractors must be sensitive to the effects of noise, odor, light, fugitive dust emissions and traffic movement to the organization and the local community. Contractors shall be required to prepare and maintain Documented Information pertaining to the work performed in accordance with environmental regulatory requirements, including record retention requirements. Contractors shall *ensure protection of the natural environment surrounding all work areas.*

*Contractors shall ensure that all employees are properly trained on such things as the proper handling of material and equipment, proper response to incidents involving their material and general information relating to **[Organization's Name]**'s EMS.*

Environmental Management System Documented Information

***[Organization's Name]**'s may wish to include or provide the following information prior to contractors and subcontractors beginning work: Environmental Policy; Index of Environmental Management System Procedures and Index of local Procedures and Work Instructions.*

Resource 50 Contractor Work Method Statement

The contractor shall prepare and maintain information including a clear Method Statement, regarding contractor and sub-contractor activities, which outlines the work to be undertaken and the method(s) for minimizing Environmental Impacts and maintaining compliance with environmental regulations.

Note to reader: To assist in organizing and maintaining information, background information sections have been included in Sections I, II and III. These Sections can be modified or deleted as required when requesting your own Method Statements from Contractors.

[Organization's Name]'s Personnel are to complete Sections I, II, and III and Contractor or Supplier staff are to complete Section IV.

Section I. Your information:

Include your Name, Phone number, Email, Dept Name and Dept Number

Section II. Requisition Information:

Include the Requisition Number and Project number

Section III. Service or Activity to be performed:

In clued details of the organization's department where work is to be done and the type of activity.

Section IV. Supplier/Contractor information:

The Supplier/Contractor is either (state 'yes' or 'no'):

A new Supplier/Contractor to this Organization: yes or no?

Currently involved in other Organization project(s): yes or no?

If the Supplier/Contractor is currently involved in other Organization project please list the project(s):

Supplier/Contractor to supply the following information about themselves:

Name	Organization site coordinator name
Address	
Email	Organization site coordinator email
Phone number	
General Manager	Organization site coordinator phone number
	24 hour emergency number

Which of the following types of activity is the Supplier/Contractor undertaking on site?

- Architectural
- Mechanical
- Electrical
- HVAC
- Industrial Services
- Painting
- Roofing
- Asbestos
- Architectural/Engineering
- Consulting Firm
- Sampling/Testing
- Chemical Supplier
- Other (specify)
- Scrap/Salvage Dealer
- Waste Disposal
- Demolition Disposal

The Supplier/Contractor is financially responsible for on-site environmental remediation actions resulting from incidents involving their employees and subcontractors.

Environmental Management whilst working on site

Suppliers/Contractors to agree to these points before work starts. Supplier/Contractor understands the importance of compliance with relevant environmental legislation and regulations and the consequences of non-compliance. All Suppliers/Contractors working at the organization are required to comply with and ensure that their employees and any Suppliers or Sub-Contractors comply with the organization's EMS and Environmental Policy. All

Suppliers/Contractors acknowledge receiving or were made aware of the organization's Environmental Policy as well as applicable System Procedures. Suppliers/Contractors shall not discharge anything to drains or sewers without approval from the organization's EMS Coordinator. Spills must be immediately reported to the Safety Committee Champion. Suppliers/Contractors shall provide adequate spill prevention as approved by the organization's EMS Coordinator. Suppliers/Contractors shall immediately notify the organization's EMS Coordinator and the Project Manager of any abnormal conditions found during excavations at the organization. Suppliers/Contractors shall properly label, store and dispose of all their waste materials used on-site in accordance with organization procedures and all legal requirements. If organization personnel are required to work with potentially hazardous materials brought on-site by a contractor, prior approval of the material by the EMS Coordinator is required. Suppliers/Contractors shall minimize the effects of noise, odor, light, fugitive dust emissions and traffic movement on or adjacent to organization property. Suppliers/Contractors shall obtain, prior to commencing work, all necessary environmental approvals or permits and present copies of such permits to the organization's EMS Coordinator. Suppliers/Contractors were informed of actions to be taken during an emergency situation. The Supplier/Contractor understands that the organization may interrupt their activities that violate organization policies or compliance requirements.

Air Emissions

Will the work you perform produce or cause the release of any air emissions? If so, list air emissions and method for preventing impact to the environment.

Water Discharges

Will the work you perform produce or cause the release of any wastewater? If so, how will the wastewater be handled?

Materials

What materials or equipment will you be bringing on-site?

Training

Your employees should be trained on the proper handling of materials and equipment and the proper response to incidents involving these materials. Describe the training your employees receive.

Waste Generation

If the work you perform results in wastes, list the disposal location as well as amounts and types of wastes expected and the proposed disposal method. Will any wastes generated be recyclable? If so, list the recyclable and where and how they will be recycled.

Energy

Will the work you perform consume energy? If so, explain what type of energy will be consumed, and how you will minimize consumption.

Other

Are there any other ways in which your work will be affecting and/or protecting the environment? If so, please describe.

Identify environmental legal requirements applicable to the work that was not already addressed by the organization.

28 APPENDIX 13: PROCEDURE FOR EMERGENCY PREPAREDNESS AND RESPONSE

PURPOSE

This Procedure defines the framework for preparing for and responding to emergencies involving potential environmental incidents at **[Organization's Name]**.

ACTIVITIES AFFECTED

All areas and departments

FORMS USED

Resource 36 Questions, the answers to which help in the development and maintenance of Emergency Preparedness and Response Plans and Procedures

Resource 37 Emergency Preparedness and Response Requirements checklist

REFERENCES

Appendix 4: Procedure for Environmental Aspects, Objectives, and Action Plans

Appendix 8: Procedure for Communicating With Stakeholders

Appendix 15: Procedure for Corrective Action

ISO 14001: clause 8.2.

EXCLUSIONS

None

PROCEDURE

Potential environmental incidents and emergencies likely to occur at the organization shall be identified semi-annually by the Cross Functional Team and recorded according to this Emergency Preparedness and Response Procedure.

Methods to respond to, mitigate and prevent environmental emergencies shall be established and maintained at the organization in the Security Office by the Emergency Response Coordinator.

Roles and responsibilities for communications within the organization and for obtaining outside support services shall be established and maintained at the organization via Emergency Plans.

Environmental emergency methods and communications will be tested at least annually. The Security Office shall maintain Documented Information of these tests. Methods to respond to, mitigate and prevent environmental emergencies shall be amended as required based on the results of these tests.

Following an environmental emergency, the cause of the emergency and corresponding emergency methods shall be reviewed. Methods to respond to, mitigate and prevent incidents that arise as a consequence of an environmental emergency shall be amended as required and the Environmental Management Representative or EMS Coordinator notified.

GENERAL RULES

All emergency response activities are to be conducted within boundaries of training levels, appropriate Procedures and governmental regulations.

The Organization Manager shall designate an Emergency Response Coordinator.

DOCUMENTED INFORMATION

Documents shall be retained consistent with the Procedure for Environmental Documented Information.

RECORD OF REVISIONS

Describe the revision made, the date of the change and the sections of the Procedure affected.

29 Appendix 14: Procedure for Monitoring, Measurement, Analysis and Evaluation

Purpose

This Procedure defines the mechanism for the monitoring, measurement, analysis and evaluation of Significant Environmental Aspects associated with **[Organization's Name]**'s operations and activities, the calibration and maintenance of monitoring equipment and the evaluation of compliance with relevant obligations, including policy requirements.

Activities Affected

All areas and departments

References

Appendix 2: Procedure for Identification of Compliance Obligations

Appendix 4: Procedure for Environmental Aspects, Objectives, and Action Plans

Appendix 8: Procedure for Communicating With Stakeholders

ISO 14001: clause 9.1.

Procedure

The monitoring and measurement of key characteristics and the environmental performance associated with Significant Aspects will be specified in Environmental Management Programs.

The monitoring, measurement, analysis and evaluation of conformance will be accomplished through the internal system audit process and through the creation of Corrective Action Requests.

Operational Controls will be monitored, measured, analysed and evaluated as indicated in applicable Environmental Management Programs, Procedures, work practices or visual aids. The methods, frequencies and responsible parties for completing the monitoring, measurement, analysis and evaluation activities will be specified.

Calibration and Maintenance of Environmental Monitoring Equipment

Relevant areas and departments shall ensure that environmental monitoring equipment is calibrated and maintained at a frequency consistent with manufacturers' recommendations, or at least every year if those recommendations are unknown. Relevant areas and departments shall maintain calibration and maintenance Documented Information as necessary to prove conformance with this procedure.

Calibration and maintenance of environmental monitoring equipment shall be addressed in area and department preventative maintenance programs or in local work practices.

Each applicable area and department will maintain a list of EMS equipment requiring calibration and the corresponding calibration frequency.

Evaluation of Compliance

The evaluation of compliance with relevant environmental legal and other Compliance Obligations shall be accomplished through the implementation of Procedures for Environmental Management System and Regulatory Compliance Audits.

FREQUENCY

Ongoing

DOCUMENTED INFORMATION

Documents shall be retained consistent with the Procedure for Environmental Documented Information.

RECORD OF REVISIONS

Describe the revision made, the date of the change and the sections of the Procedure affected.

30 APPENDIX 15: PROCEDURE FOR CORRECTIVE ACTION

PURPOSE

The purpose of this Procedure is to establish and outline the process for identifying, documenting, analyzing and implementing preventive and corrective actions. Preventive or corrective actions may be initiated using this Procedure for any environmental problem affecting the organization.

ACTIVITIES AFFECTED

All areas and departments

FORMS USED

Resource 34 Corrective Action Request

Resource 35 Corrective Action Tracking Log

REFERENCES

Appendix 8: Procedure for Communicating With Stakeholders

Appendix 11: Procedure for Document Control

Appendix 13: Procedure for Emergency Preparedness and Response

Appendix 14: Procedure for Monitoring, Measurement, Analysis and Evaluation

Appendix 16: Procedure for EMS and Regulatory and other Compliance Obligations Audits

ISO 14001: clause 10.2.

PROCEDURE

Where non-compliances are identified through the environmental audit process, the responsible and accountable area or department representative, affected area or department manager, audit team member or Environmental Management Representative (EMR), is responsible for:

- Identifying the root cause(s) of non-compliances.
- Identifying appropriate corrective actions (including modifying or creating environmental procedures and work practices).
- Planning and implementing corrective actions.
- Verifying the completion, and effectiveness, of corrective actions.
- Where non-conformances are identified outside the environmental audit process, the Environmental Manager or designee will generate a Corrective Action Request. The affected area or department manager is responsible for:

- Identifying the root cause(s) of these non-compliances.
- Identifying appropriate corrective actions (including modifying or creating Environmental Procedures and work practices).
- Planning and implementing corrective actions.
- Verifying the close-out and effectiveness of corrective actions.

The Quality Manager will verify proper implementation of corrective actions.

Frequency

As needed following Reviews.

Documented Information

Documents shall be retained consistent with the Procedure for Environmental Documented Information.

Record of Revisions

Describe the revision made, the date of the change and the sections of the Procedure affected.

31 APPENDIX 16: PROCEDURE FOR EMS AND REGULATORY AND OTHER COMPLIANCE OBLIGATIONS AUDITS

PURPOSE

This Procedure defines the mechanism for the planning and implementation of internal Environmental Management System and regulatory compliance audits at **[Organization's Name]**.

ACTIVITIES AFFECTED

All areas and departments

FORMS USED

Resource 34 Corrective Action Request

Resource 41 Help in developing an organization's Audit Procedure

Resource 42 Questions, the answers to which can help you to determine your organization's audit Procedure

Resource 46 Legal and Compliance Obligations identification

Resource 47 Example Index of Environmental Documented Information

REFERENCES

Appendix 15: Procedure for Corrective Action

Appendix 17: Procedure for EMS Management Review

ISO 14001: clause 9.2.2 and 7.5.2.

PROCEDURE

Conducting the Internal EMS Audit

The Environmental Manager (although this is sometimes delegated to the Quality Manager) shall plan, schedule and implement internal EMS audits. The audit schedule will be used to identify the frequency and location of internal EMS audits and will be revised as necessary. Revisions to the audit schedule may be based on the results of prior audits.

Audit frequency will be established taking into account previous audit results and the relative importance of the area or department and will not be less that once per year for each location. Each area or department will be audited at least once every three years on all System elements.

For each area or department within the organization an audit team will be formed whose members have no responsibility within the area or department to be audited. This independence will be recorded by indicating on the audit report or other audit Documented Information the department or organization to which the auditors belong.

Competency of audit teams

At least one member of the team shall be competent in the environmental auditing process through either training or experience.

All members of the audit team shall have an awareness and understanding of **[Organization's Name]**'s Environmental Management System from formal and informal training.

Audit scope and criteria will be established for each area or department prior to each audit. Audit criteria may be documented by the audit team on an Internal EMS Audit Checklist and the checklist used during the audits.

During the audit the audit team will record audit information, such as items checked; individuals interviewed; any concerns identified and any corrective actions completed during the audit. The audit team shall promptly notify the Environmental Management Representative (EMR) of any possible regulatory non-compliance. Upon verification of non-compliance the EMR shall notify the organization's senior managers.

Upon completion of the internal audit the audit team will review their findings with the auditee and responsible and accountable area or department representative. The team will then initiate a Corrective Action Request, (CAR) for each finding of non-conformance using the CAR form.

The Environmental Manager will track the status of all outstanding CAR's using the Corrective Action Tracking Log.

The responsible and accountable area or department representative will identify the root cause of the non-conformance and corrective actions to be undertaken and the dates by which these actions will be completed. This information will be documented on the original CAR and the CAR sent to the applicable area or department manager. A copy of the CAR will also be provided to the Environmental Manager within the time frame established during the audit review meeting.

Upon completion of the corrective actions the area or department manager will acknowledge completion of these actions by signing the original CAR and returning it to the Environmental Manager.

Corrective actions will be verified during the next internal audit or the area or department manager may contact the Environmental Manager to schedule verification of actions prior to the next audit.

When full conformance is determined or Corrective Actions accepted, the audit team leader will sign the original CAR and return it to the Environmental Manager for closure and filing.

At least annually, the EMR will summarize system audit results with organization management as specified in the Procedure for Environmental Management System Management Review.

Conducting the Compliance Assessment Audit

The EMR is responsible for planning, scheduling and implementing internal environmental regulatory compliance assessment audits, including the identification of required resources.

The EMR develops and maintains the Environmental Compliance Assurance Program and issues program support Documented Information, based on organization environmental compliance assurance guidelines, where available.

During a compliance assessment audit, assessment team members will record information such as items checked; individuals interviewed and any possible regulatory non-compliance issues. The assessment team shall promptly notify the EMR of any possible regulatory non-compliance. Upon verification of non-compliance the EMR shall notify the organization's senior managers.

The assessment team reviews possible regulatory non-compliance issues with the responsible and accountable area or department representative. The team also prepares a CAR identifying the issues, corrective actions required and the individuals responsible for completing the actions. The EMR and area or department manager will agree with the CAR before it is issued.

Upon completion of the corrective actions, the area or department manager will acknowledge completion of these actions by signing the original CAR and returning it to the EMR.

Corrective actions will be verified in a timely manner by a member of the assessment team. When full compliance is determined or corrective actions accepted the assessment team member will sign the original CAR and return it to the EMR for closure and filing.

Every three months the EMR will present to the organization's senior managers for review a summary of CARs still to be completed and which are based on regulatory non-compliance.

FREQUENCY

At least annually

DOCUMENTED INFORMATION

Documents shall be retained consistent with the Procedure for Environmental Documented Information.

RECORD OF REVISIONS

Describe the revision made, the date of the change and the sections of the Procedure affected.

32 APPENDIX 17: PROCEDURE FOR EMS MANAGEMENT REVIEW

PURPOSE

This Procedure defines the process for the periodic review and evaluation of **[Organization's Name]**'s Environmental Management System by senior managers to ensure its continuing suitability, adequacy and effectiveness.

ACTIVITIES AFFECTED

All areas and departments

FORMS USED

Resource 42 Questions, the answers to which can help you to determine your organization's audit Procedure

Resource 44 EMS Management Review Record

REFERENCES

Appendix 2: Procedure for Identification of Compliance Obligations

Appendix 4: Procedure for Environmental Aspects, Objectives, and Action Plans

Appendix 14: Procedure for Monitoring, Measurement, Analysis and Evaluation

Appendix 15: Procedure for Corrective Action

Appendix 16: Procedure for EMS and Regulatory and other Compliance Obligations Audits

ISO 14001: clause 9.3

PROCEDURE

The Site Manager and senior managers shall conduct a review of the EMS at least once each year.

Management Review meetings shall be scheduled in advance by the Environmental Management Representative (EMR) and an agenda issued to ensure appropriate preparation and attendance.

The meeting shall review all applicable components of **[Organization's Name]**'s EMS. The EMR shall present information for review which may include:

- Environmental Policy.
- Environmental Aspects.
- Objectives and Programs.
- Compliance Obligations.
- Training and Competence.
- Operational Control.

- Emergency Preparedness and Response.
- Monitoring and Measurement.
- Non-conformance mitigation actions.
- Environmental System and Compliance Audits.

The Site Manager and senior managers shall review and confirm their approval and the continual suitability, adequacy and effectiveness of the Environmental Policy, Environmental Objectives, Environmental Management Programs, and other elements of the System as well as confirm that Compliance Obligations are met.

The EMR will publish and maintain meeting minutes identifying issues discussed and corrective actions to be taken, as well as:

- Conclusions on EMS' suitability, adequacy & effectiveness
- Decisions about improvement opportunities
- Decisions about need for changes to EMS
- Actions to achieve Environmental Objectives
- Opportunities for better EMS integration with business processes
- Implications for organizational strategy

Required actions will be assigned to the responsibility of process, area and functional management

Documented Information

Documents shall be retained consistent with the Procedure for Environmental Documented information.

Record of Revisions

Describe the revision made, the date of the change and the sections of the Procedure affected.